Folksy FAVORITES

Tip your hat to days gone by with our collection of folksy sampler quilts. Designer Pat Sloan uses playful appliqués and rustic prints to create seven sentimental quilts and wall hangings. From the fanciful "Love Letters" to the endearing "Ma-Ma's Garden," you'll be captivated by the "storytelling" quality of Pat's primitive quilts. Seasonal samplers like "Harvest Moon," "I Believe," and "Slice of Summer" perfectly depict the essence of autumn, winter, and summer. Greet visitors with a "Heartfelt Welcome" wall hanging, or find comfort in a "Basket of Hope" (designed in the days following September 11, 2001). So grab your scrap basket and get ready to create your own cherished folk-art quilt!

LEISURE ARTS, INC.
Little Rock, Arkansas

Table of Contents

Meet Pat Sloan

For designer Pat Sloan, quilting has "shaped up" into an occupation she never would have dreamed of pursuing.

Although Pat grew up sewing and crafting (she jokes that she's sewn "since I could find a needle in the house"), she didn't start quilting until a friend persuaded her to take a class 10 years ago. "At first I thought it would be boring," Pat admits, "but she signed me up, and I haven't looked back."

Since then, quilting has become Pat's favorite activity, in part because she enjoys working with her hands. "I like that motion, the action of creating something, especially with fabric," she says. "I've tried all the crafts ... and cloth is my favorite."

This enthusiasm for quilting led Pat, a former computer programmer who worked in human resources, to quit her job five years ago. Her experience teaching quilting classes and creating models for a local quilt shop convinced her that she wanted to spend her time quilting.

Designing was almost an afterthought. "I just had to find a way to quilt full-time," Pat says. "I started designing because I had to choose something that I could develop very quickly."

Though she may seem brave for her willingness to step out and carve a new path for herself, Pat admits that she was actually very nervous at the thought of quitting her job. "I'm conservative. I'd never done anything like that before!" she confesses. But her husband, Gregg, gave her the extra encouragement she needed, telling her to "just go for it." And as the business has grown, Gregg has shown his support once again, by quitting his own job to work full-time in the quilting industry, too. "He does all the printing, editing, shipping ... everything but color and design!" Pat laughs.

Design has indeed remained Pat's domain, and the ideas seem to flow naturally from the converted living room where she spends most of her working day. Her style tends toward old-fashioned, yet whimsical, quilts and wall hangings — not surprising since she finds much of her inspiration in old Baltimore appliqué quilts, which she feels have "lots of personality." Many of Pat's own quilts display a variety of free-form appliqués. "I like big, simple shapes. I like the freedom of having no structure," she explains.

Pat's designs are also inspired by the simple style of the Amish. Although she spent most of her childhood in New Jersey, Germany, and Belgium, Pat often visited relatives who lived near Amish Country in Pennsylvania. She loved the distinct Pennsylvania Dutch art as a child and has seen its influence in her own unique folk-art style.

Whatever its influences, Pat's quilting style has caught on. A little over two years ago, Pat started her own company, Pat Sloan & Co., which designs and publishes patterns for quilts, penny rugs, and rug hooking.

Pat currently divides her time between designing, managing her company, and teaching workshops and seminars on quilting (about 10 per year). She hopes to teach more classes in the future, as well as develop more books and design a fabric line.

When asked what she attributes her success to, Pat responds, "I believed I could do it ... I enjoy what I do, and hopefully other people enjoy it, too."

Heartfelt Welcome

Like a basket of fresh-picked wildflowers, friends fill our lives with a serendipitous mixture of beauty and delight. Welcome these much-loved guests into your home with a winsome wall hanging that symbolizes the charm they bring to your world. Floral-print fabrics add a touch of fun to your flower appliqués.

HEARTFELT WELCOME
Finished Size: 41¹/₂" x 36¹/₂" (105 x 93 cm)

FABRIC REQUIREMENTS
¹/₂ yd (46 cm) of tan print No. 1
¹/₂ yd (46 cm) of tan print No. 2
⁵/₈ yd (57 cm) of black print No. 1
1¹/₈ yds (1.1 m) of black print No. 2
¹/₄ yd (23 cm) of black print No. 3
¹/₄ yd (23 cm) of assorted blue prints
¹/₄ yd (23 cm) of assorted pale gold prints
³/₈ yd (34 cm) of assorted red prints
³/₄ yd (69 cm) of green print No. 1
¹/₄ yd (23 cm) of green print No. 2
³/₄ yd (69 cm) of binding fabric
1³/₈ yds (1.3 m) of backing fabric
45¹/₂" x 40¹/₂" (116 x 103 cm) batting

CUTTING THE BACKGROUNDS AND BORDERS
*Yardage is based on 45"w fabric. Refer to **Rotary Cutting**, page 102, before beginning project.*
From tan print No. 1:
  • Cut 2 background rectangles 14¹/₂" x 12".
From tan print No. 2:
  • Cut 2 background rectangles 14¹/₂" x 12".
From black print No. 1:
  • Cut 2 lengthwise top/bottom inner borders 28¹/₂" x 1".
  • Cut 2 lengthwise side inner borders 24¹/₂" x 1".
From black print No. 2:
  • Cut 2 lengthwise top/bottom outer borders 29¹/₂" x 6¹/₄".
  • Cut 2 lengthwise side outer borders 36" x 6¹/₄".

CUTTING THE APPLIQUÉS

Refer to **Making Templates**, page 104, to use patterns, pages 7-13, to make templates. **Note:** Appliqué patterns provided do not include seam allowances.
From green print No. 1:
- Cut 2 bias strips 1¹/₂" x 16" for stems (A).
- Cut 2 bias strips 1¹/₂" x 15" for stems (B).
- Cut 1 bias strip 1¹/₂" x 7" for stem (C).
- Cut 1 lower left stem (D).
- Cut 1 lower right stem (E1 and E2).
- Cut 2 bias strips 1¹/₂" x 33" for stems (O).

From black print No. 3:
- Cut 1 basket handle (F) on fold.
- Cut 1 basket (G) on fold.

From black print No. 1:
- Cut 1 bias strip 1¹/₂" x 18¹/₂" for basket rim (H).
- Cut 3 berry centers (N).

From assorted pale gold prints:
- Cut 2 stars (P).
- Cut 3 flower centers (K).
- Cut 3 berry centers (N).
- Cut the letters "WELCOME".

From assorted blue prints:
- Cut 2 stars (P).
- Cut 1 heart (L).

From assorted red prints:
- Cut 3 flowers (J).
- Cut 9 berries (M); 2 are used for star centers and 1 is used for heart center.

From green print No. 2:
- Cut 14 leaves (I).

ASSEMBLING THE QUILT TOP

Note: Some of the appliqués on this quilt extend beyond the edges of the background blocks onto the borders. The borders may be sewn to background blocks before appliquéing, or the appliqué edges that extend may be left unstitched (pin edges out of the way) until the borders are attached.

1. Refer to **Piecing and Pressing**, page 103, to sew the 4 background rectangles together.
2. Sew the top and bottom inner borders to the quilt top, then add the side inner borders. Sew the top and bottom outer borders to the quilt top, then the side outer borders.
3. Refer to **Appliqué**, page 105, for techniques. Our quilt was appliquéd using the **Needleturn Appliqué** method. Refer to **Quilt Top Diagram**, page 8, and photo, page 6, for placement. Working in alphabetical order, position pieces, then pin or baste in place before appliquéing.

FINISHING

1. Follow **Quilting**, page 107, to mark, layer, and quilt as desired. Our quilt has freeform machine quilting in the background and border. The flowers, stars, berry centers, and heart are outlined quilted inside the shape. The leaves and stems are not quilted.
2. Cut a 22" square of binding fabric. Follow **Binding**, page 110, to bind quilt using 2¹/₂"w bias binding with mitered corners.
3. Refer to **Making a Hanging Sleeve**, page 112, to make and attach a hanging sleeve.

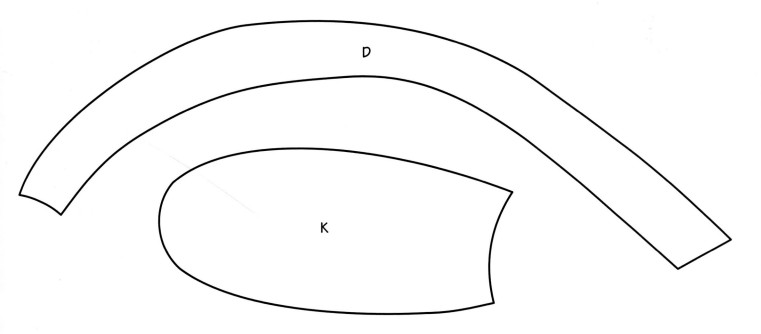

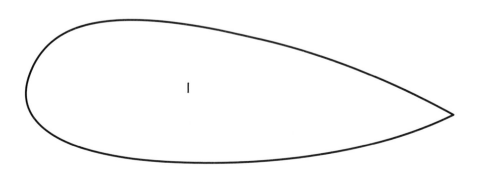

1

8

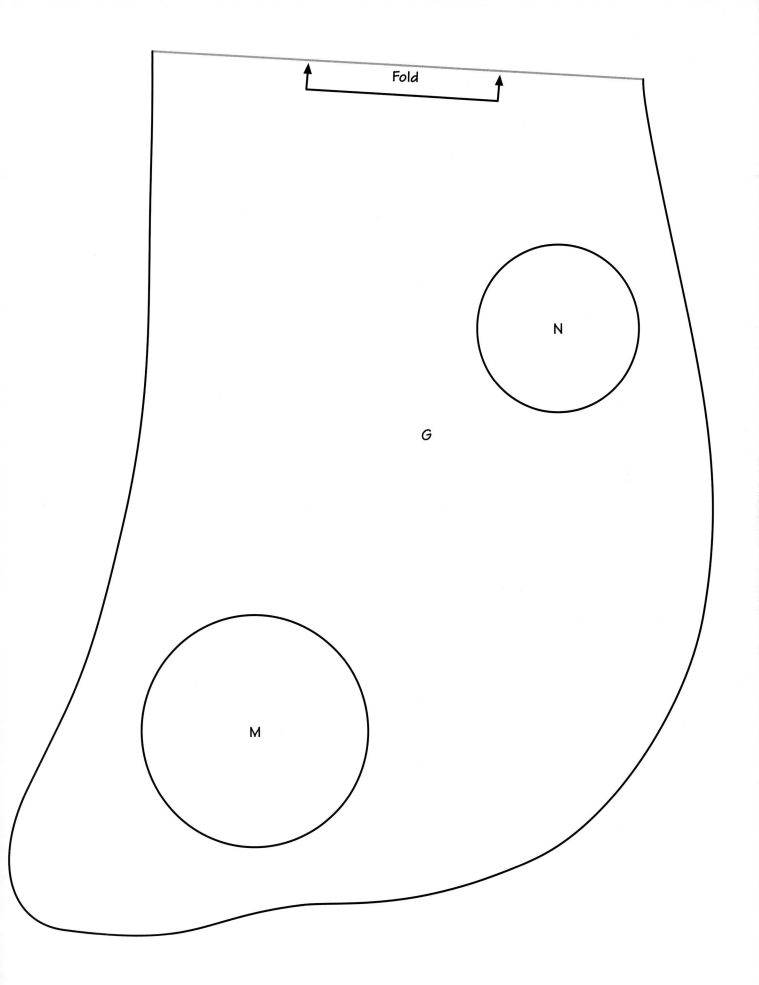

Fold

N

G

M

Fold

F

P

J

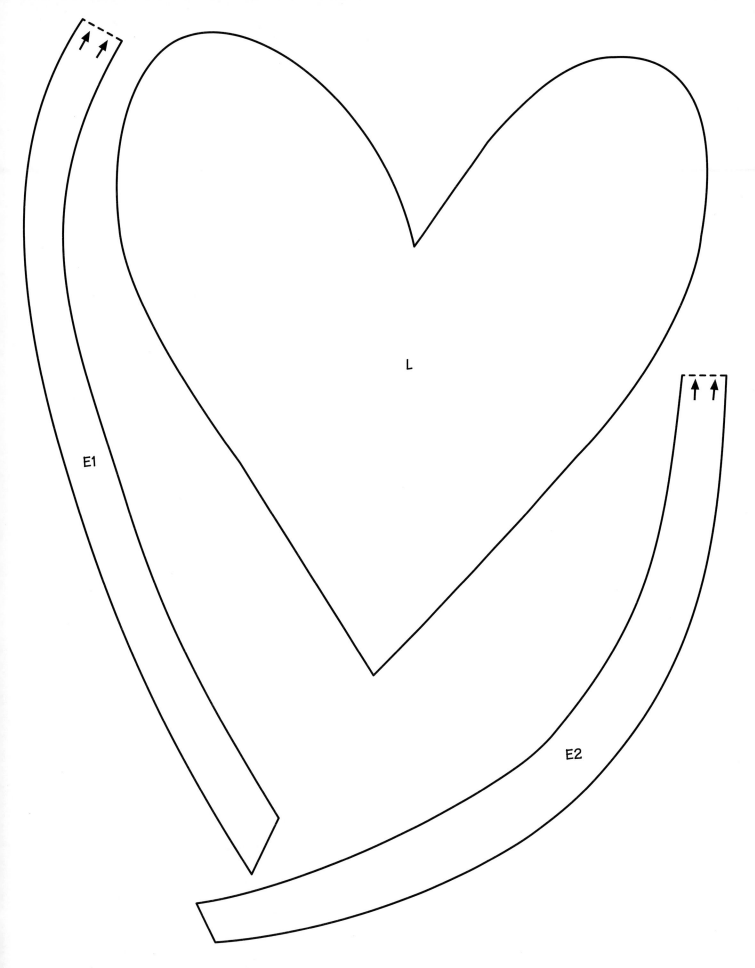

E1

L

E2

Love ♥ Letters

From the moment Cupid's arrow first pierces your heart, the whole world seems to glow with love. More than 20 heart-shaped appliqués, including a romantic bouquet, a cherished love letter, and a string of X's and O's, evoke memories of youth's first love and echo promises of happily ever after.

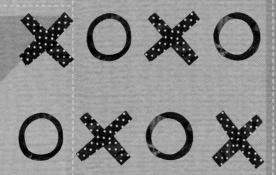

LOVE LETTERS
Finished Size: 50" x 53" (127 x 135 cm)

FABRIC REQUIREMENTS

1¼ yds (1.1 m) of assorted cream prints
1½ yds (1.4 m) of assorted tan prints
¾ yd (69 cm) of assorted green prints
⅜ yd (34 cm) of dark red print
1⅜ yd (1.3 m) of red floral print
½ yd (46 cm) of assorted red prints
¼ yd (23 cm) of blue polka dot
¼ yd (23 cm) of blue floral print
¾ yd (69 cm) of assorted blue prints
¼ yd (23 cm) of gold print
¾ yd (69 cm) binding fabric
3½ yds (3.2 m) backing fabric
54" x 57" (137 x 145 cm) rectangle of batting

CUTTING THE BACKGROUNDS, SASHINGS, AND BORDERS

*Yardage is based on 45"w fabric. Refer to **Rotary Cutting**, page 102, before beginning project. To help keep pieces organized, refer to **Quilt Assembly Diagram**, page 21, to lay out the pieces as you cut.*

From assorted cream prints:
- Cut 2 squares (No. 1) 12½" x 12½".
- Cut 1 rectangle (No. 2) 19½" x 6½".
- Cut 1 rectangle (No. 3) 10½" x 5½".
- Cut 1 square (No. 4) 10½" x 10½".
- Cut 1 rectangle (No. 5) 8½" x 18½".
- Cut 4 squares (No. 6) 3½" x 3½".
- Cut 1 rectangle (No. 7) 5½" x 8½".
- Cut 1 rectangle (No. 8) 28½" x 8½".

From assorted tan prints:
- Cut 20 squares (No. 9) 2½" x 2½".
- Cut 2 rectangles (No. 10) 5½" x 1½".
- Cut 4 rectangles (No. 11) 3½" x 2½".
- Cut 4 rectangles (No. 12) 12½" x 2½".
- Cut 2 rectangles (No. 13) 9" x 2½".
- Cut 4 rectangles (No. 14) 7" x 2½".
- Cut 2 rectangles (No. 15) 10" x 2½".
- Cut 120 squares 2⅞" x 2⅞". Cut squares once diagonally to make 240 triangles.

From assorted green prints:
- Cut 2 rectangles (No. 17) 5½" x 1½".
- Cut 1 rectangle (No. 18) 8½" x 2½".
- Cut 2 rectangles (No. 19) 3½" x 1½".
- Cut 2 rectangles (No. 20) 8½" x 1½".
- Cut 2 rectangles (No. 21) 10½" x 1½".
- Cut 1 rectangle (No. 22) 12½" x 1½".

From red floral print:
- Cut 2 lengthwise strips, piecing as necessary, 2" x 46½" for side inner borders.
- Cut 2 lengthwise strips, piecing as necessary, 2" x 46½" for the top and bottom inner borders.

From assorted blue prints:
- Cut 120 squares 2⅞" x 2⅞". Cut squares once diagonally to make 240 triangles.

CUTTING THE APPLIQUÉS

*Refer to **Making Templates**, page 104, to use patterns, pages 23-25, to make templates. **Note:** Appliqué patterns provided do not include seam allowances. Measurements given for rectangles include a ¼" seam allowance. To help keep blocks organized, lay out all appliqué pieces with corresponding backgrounds as you cut.*

Crossed Hearts
From assorted green prints:
- Cut 2 stems 1" x 11" (A).
- Cut 8 leaves (B).

From assorted red prints:
- Cut 5 hearts (C).

Lovebirds
From assorted green prints:
- Cut 1 stem, cut 1 in reverse (D).
- Cut 2 stems; cut 2 in reverse (E).

From assorted red prints:
- Cut 4 hearts (F).

From gold print:
- Cut 2 flower centers (G).

From blue floral print:
- Cut 2 flowers (H).

From dark red print:
- Cut 1 lovebird; cut 1 in reverse (I).

Love Letter
From blue print:
- Cut 1 envelope bottom 8½" x 3½" (J).

From blue polka dot:
- Cut 1 envelope flap (K).

From a red print:
- Cut 1 envelope heart (L).

Feathered Heart
From dark red print:
- Cut 1 heart on fold (M).
- Cut 1 heart (C).

From assorted green prints:
- Cut 13 leaves (B).

From gold print:
- Cut 1 dot (N).

Wreath
From assorted green prints:
- Cut 1 wreath (O) on fold.
- Cut 4 leaves; cut 4 in reverse (P).

From assorted red prints:
- Cut 4 small hearts (L).
- Cut 4 dots (N).

From gold print:
- Cut 4 dots (N).
- Cut 1 heart (C).

Vase
From blue floral print:
- Cut 1 vase (Q).

From assorted green prints:
- Cut 3 stems (R).
- Cut 6 leaves (S).

From assorted red prints:
- Cut 3 hearts (T).

From gold print:
- Cut 3 dots (N).

Hugs and Kisses
From blue polka dot:
- Cut 4 kiss strips (U).

From a red print:
- Cut 2 hugs (V).

Lace Heart
From a blue print:
- Cut 1 scalloped heart (W).

From a red print:
- Cut 1 heart (X).

Heart Vine
From a red print:
- Cut 1 large heart (Y) on fold.

From assorted green prints:
- Cut 1 stem; cut 1 in reverse (Z).
- Cut 10 leaves (AA).

MAKING THE BLOCKS
*Refer to **Needleturn Appliqué**, page 105, for technique. Refer to the **Block Diagrams** and photo for placement.* **Note:** *Some of the appliqués on this quilt extend beyond the edges of their background blocks onto the sashing strips. The sashing strips may be sewn to background blocks before appliquéing, or the appliqué edges that extend may be left unstitched (pin edges out of the way) until the sashing strips are attached.*

Triangle-Squares for Sashing and Border
1. Refer to **Piecing and Pressing**, page 103, to **Chain Piece** blue and tan triangles to make 239 Triangle-Squares (**Unit 1**).

Unit 1 (make 239)

2. Sew 2 Unit 1's together to make 79 Flying Geese Blocks (**Unit 2**).

Unit 2 (make 79)

Crossed Hearts
1. Appliqué 2 A's, 8 B's, and 5 C's onto a No. 1 background block.
2. Sew 3 Unit 2's together to make a Sashing Strip. Make 4.
3. Sew 1 Sashing Strip to the top and the bottom of the block.
4. Sew 1 square (No. 9) to each end of the remaining Sashing Strips. Sew 1 Sashing Strip to each side of the block.

Crossed Hearts Diagram

Lovebirds

1. Appliqué 2 D's, 4 E's, 4 F's, 2 G's, 2 H's, and 2 I's onto the No. 2 background block.
2. Sew 3 Unit 2's together to make a Sashing Strip. Make 2. Sew 1 Sashing Strip to each side of the block.

Lovebirds Diagram

Love Letter

1. Appliqué 1 J, 1 K, and 1 L onto the No. 3 background block.
2. Sew a No. 17 strip, then a No. 10 strip to each side of the block.

Love Letter Diagram

Feathered Heart

1. Appliqué 1 M, 1 C, 13 B's and 1 N onto a No. 1 background block.
2. Sew 3 Unit 2's together to make a Sashing Strip. Make 4.
3. Sew 1 Sashing Strip to the top and bottom of the block.
4. Sew 1 square (No. 9) to each end of the remaining Sashing Strips. Sew 1 Sashing Strip to each side of the block.
5. Sew 4 Unit 1's and 2 Unit 2's together. Sew to bottom edge of block.

Feathered Heart Diagram

Wreath

1. Appliqué 1 O, 8 P's, 4 L's, 4 red and 4 gold N's, and 1 C to the No. 4 background block.
2. Sew 5 Unit 1's together to make a Sashing Strip. Make 4.
3. Sew 1 Sashing Strip to the top and bottom of the block.
4. Sew 1 square (No. 9) to each end of the remaining Sashing Strips. Sew 1 Sashing Strip to each side of the block.

Wreath Diagram

Vase

1. Appliqué 1 Q, 3 R's, 6 S's, 3 T's, and 3 N's onto the No. 5 background block.
2. Sew 1 No. 18 rectangle to the bottom of the block.
3. Sew 2 Unit 1's together to make the Top and Bottom Sashing Strips. Make 2. Sew 1 Sashing Strip to the top and bottom of the block.
4. Sew 5 Unit 2's together to make a side Sashing Strip. Make 2.
5. Sew 1 square (No. 9) to each end of the side Sashing Strip. Sew 1 Sashing Strip to each side of the block.

Vase Diagram

Hugs and Kisses

1. Appliqué 4 U's and 2 V's onto the No. 6 background blocks.
2. Sew the 4 No. 6 blocks together, alternating Hugs and Kisses.
3. Sew a No. 19 rectangle to each side of the block.
4. Sew 7 Unit 1's together to make the bottom Sashing Strip. Sew Sashing Strip to bottom edge of block.

Hugs and Kisses Diagram

Lace Heart

1. Appliqué 1 W and 1 X onto the No. 7 background block.
2. Sew 1 No. 20 rectangle to the side of block.
3. Sew 4 Unit 1's together to make the Side and Bottom Sashing Strips. Make 2. Sew Side Sashing Strip to block; sew Bottom Sashing Strip to block.
4. Sew 2 Unit 2's together to make Top Sashing Strip; sew to top edge of block.

Lace Heart Diagram

Heart Vine

1. Appliqué 1 Y, 2 Z's and 10 AA's onto the No. 8 background block.
2. Sew 7 Unit 2's together to make the Top and Bottom Sashing Strips. Make 2. Sew 1 Sashing Strip to the top and the bottom of the block.
3. Sew 2 Unit 2's together to make a side Sashing Strip. Make 2.

4. Sew 1 square (No. 9) to each end of the side Sashing Strip. Sew 1 Sashing Strip to each side of the block.

Heart Vine Diagram

Additional Sashings

1. Sew 13 Unit 2's together to make Unit 3.
2. Sew one No. 20 and two No. 21 rectangles together to make Unit 4.
3. Sew 6 Unit I's and the No. 22 together rectangle to make Unit 5.

Unit 3

Unit 4

Unit 5

ASSEMBLING THE QUILT TOP

Referring to the **Quilt Assembly Diagram** for placement, sew the blocks together in the order listed below.

1. Sew the Crossed Hearts and Feathered Heart Blocks together make Unit 6.
2. Sew the Envelope Heart, Wreath, and Hugs and Kisses Blocks together to make Unit 7.
3. Sew the Vase Block, Unit 3, Unit 4 and the Lovebirds Block to Unit 7 to make Unit 8.
4. Sew Unit 5, the Vine Heart and Lace Heart Blocks together to make Unit 9.
5. Sew Units 6, 8 and 9 together.

ADDING THE BORDERS

The Inner Border

1. Sew 1 inner border to each side of the quilt top.
2. Sew 1 inner border to the top and the bottom of the quilt top.

The Outer Border

1. For the top border, sew together 4 Unit 1's all facing the same direction; sew together 4 Unit 1's facing the opposite direction. Repeat for the bottom border.
2. Refer to **Quilt Assembly Diagram** to join Unit 4's, strips 11, 12, 13 and 14 together. Sew borders to quilt.
3. For the side border, sew together 5 Unit 1's all facing the same direction; sew together 5 Unit 1's facing the opposite direction. Repeat for the remaining side border.

4. Refer to **Assembly Diagram** to join Unit 4's, strips 11, 12, 13 and 15 together. Sew borders to quilt.

FINISHING

1. Follow **Quilting**, page 107, to mark, layer, and quilt, as desired. Our quilt is machine quilted with echo quilting around the appliqués and stipple quilting in the tan triangles and blocks.
2. Cut a 25" square of binding fabric. Follow **Binding**, page 110, to bind quilt using 2¹/₂"w bias binding with mitered corners.

Quilt Assembly Diagram

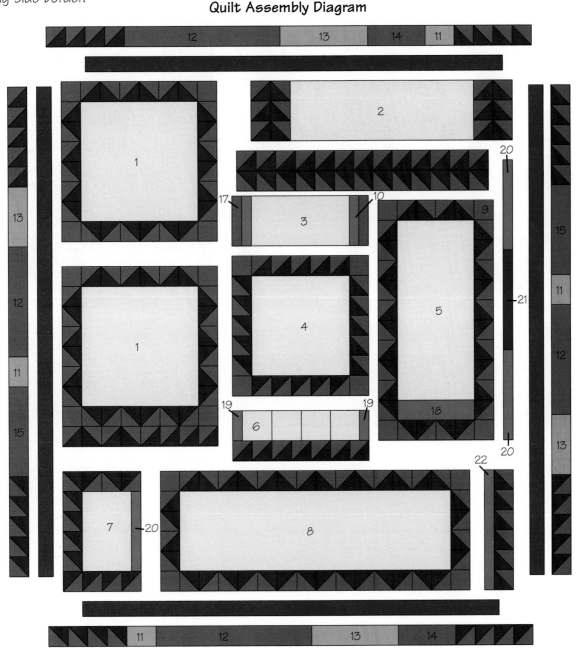

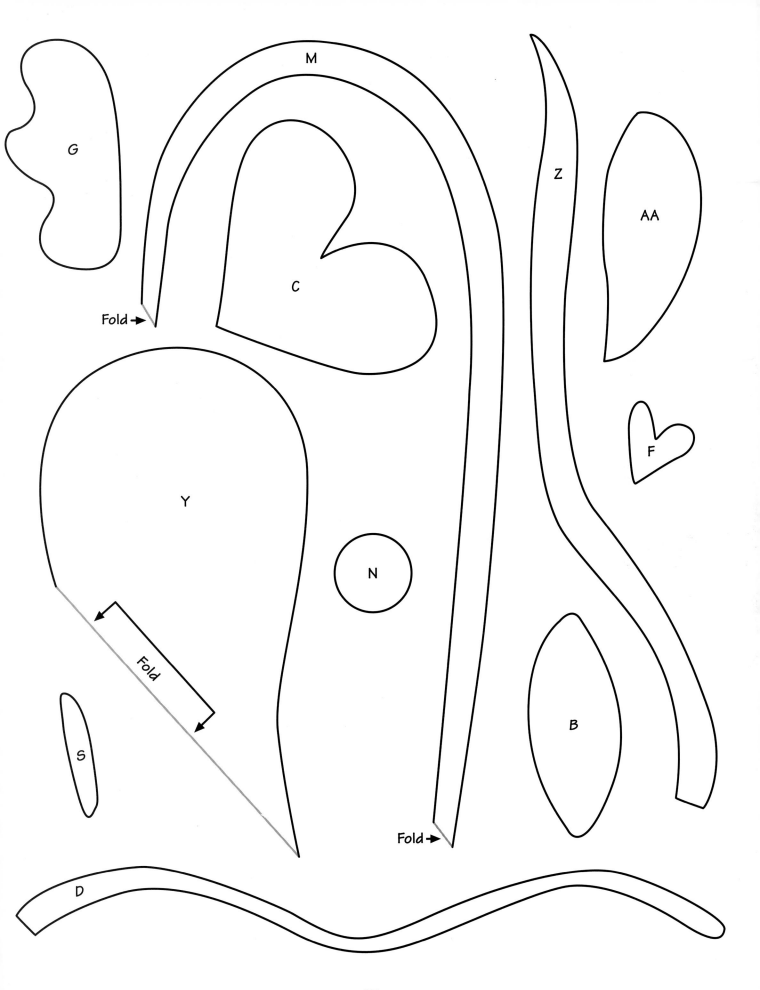

Fold

O

Fold

X

Q

T

Slice of Summer

When ladybugs and butterflies become frequent garden visitors and the sweet scent of honeysuckle fills the air, you know that summer's here. So, come on! Leave your hat on the fence and enjoy a juicy slice of watermelon while it's still cold — because this star-studded season will be over before you know it.

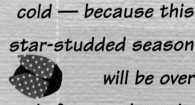

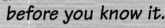

SLICE OF SUMMER
Finished Size: 37" x 45" (94 x 114 cm)

FABRIC REQUIREMENTS

$1\frac{1}{2}$ yds (1.4 m) of assorted prints with cream background

$\frac{1}{2}$ yd (46 cm) of assorted blue prints

$\frac{1}{2}$ yd (46 cm) of assorted green prints

$\frac{3}{8}$ yd (34 cm) of assorted gold prints

$\frac{1}{4}$ yd (23 cm) of assorted black prints

$\frac{1}{4}$ yd (23 cm) of assorted plum prints

Scrap of red with small cream polka dots

Scrap of small red and white stripe

Scrap of brown print

$\frac{1}{2}$ yd (46 cm) of pink print

$\frac{1}{4}$ yd (23 cm) of assorted red prints

$\frac{1}{4}$ yd (23 cm) of cream print

$1\frac{1}{4}$ yds (1.2 m) of plum print for inner border

$\frac{3}{4}$ yd (69 cm) of binding fabric

$1\frac{1}{2}$ yds (1.4 m) of backing fabric

41" x 49" (104 x 124 cm) batting

9 black buttons for watermelon seeds and crow's eye

CUTTING THE BACKGROUND AND BORDERS

Yardage is based on 45"w fabric. Refer to **Rotary Cutting**, page 102, before beginning project. To help keep pieces organized, refer to **Quilt Assembly Diagram**, page 31, to lay out the pieces as you cut.

From assorted prints with cream background:

- Cut rectangle (No. 1) 10" x $28\frac{1}{2}$".
- Cut rectangles (No. 2 and No. 3) 2" x $15\frac{1}{2}$".
- Cut rectangle (No. 4) 4" x $15\frac{1}{2}$".
- Cut rectangle (No. 5) $14\frac{1}{2}$" x $6\frac{1}{2}$".
- Cut rectangles (No. 6, No. 7, and No. 8) $14\frac{1}{2}$" x 2".
- Cut rectangles (No. 9 and No. 10) $7\frac{1}{2}$" x 5".
- Cut rectangle (No. 11) 17" x $9\frac{1}{2}$".
- Cut rectangle (No. 12) 17" x $4\frac{1}{2}$".
- Cut rectangle (No. 13) $4\frac{1}{2}$" x 6".
- Cut rectangle (No. 14) $1\frac{1}{2}$" x 8".
- Cut rectangle (No. 15) $3\frac{1}{2}$" x 8".
- Cut rectangle (No. 16) 21" x $10\frac{1}{2}$".
- Cut rectangle (No. 17) 10" x $10\frac{1}{2}$".
- Cut 38 squares $2\frac{7}{8}$" x $2\frac{7}{8}$". Cut squares in half diagonally to make 76 triangles for outer border.

From plum print for border:

- Cut 2 lengthwise top/bottom inner borders (No. 18) $1\frac{1}{2}$" x $30\frac{1}{2}$".
- Cut 2 lengthwise side inner borders (No. 19) $1\frac{1}{2}$" x $40\frac{1}{2}$".

From assorted blue prints:

- Cut 38 squares $2\frac{7}{8}$" x $2\frac{7}{8}$". Cut squares in half diagonally to make 76 triangles for outer border.

CUTTING THE APPLIQUÉS

Refer to **Making Templates**, page 104, to use patterns, pages 33-37, to make templates. **Note:** Appliqué patterns provided do not include seam allowances. Measurements given for rectangles include a $\frac{1}{4}$" seam allowance.

Honeysuckle Vine

From assorted green prints:

- Cut 5 leaves (A).

From assorted gold prints:

- Cut 9 honeysuckle flowers (B).

Ladybugs

From assorted black prints:

- Cut 3 ladybug bodies (C).

From red with small cream polka dots scrap:

- Cut 3 ladybug wings; cut 3 in reverse (D).

Americana Bunting

From assorted blue prints:

- Cut 3 bunting bottoms (E).
- Cut 4 star centers (H).

From assorted red prints:

- Cut 3 bunting tops (F).

From assorted gold prints:

- Cut 4 large stars (G).

Wave the Flag!

From assorted black prints:

- Cut 1 rectangle 1" x $5\frac{1}{2}$" for center flagpole (I).
- Cut 1 rectangle 1" x 4" for left flagpole (J).
- Cut 1 rectangle 1" x 3" for right flagpole (K).

From assorted red prints:

- Cut 1 sap bucket (L).

From cream print:

- Cut 1 rectangle 1" x 5" for top bucket stripe (M).
- Cut 1 rectangle 1" x 4" for middle bucket stripe (N).
- Cut 1 rectangle 1" x $3\frac{1}{2}$" for bottom bucket stripe (O).

From red and white stripe:

- Cut 3 rectangles 5" x $2\frac{3}{4}$" for flag stripes (P).

From assorted blue prints:

- Cut 3 squares $1\frac{3}{4}$" x $1\frac{3}{4}$" for flag fields (Q).

A Crow in the Watermelon Patch

From pink print:
- Cut 1 watermelon (R1 and R2).

From assorted green prints:
- Cut 1 watermelon rind (S1 and S2).

From assorted black prints:
- Cut 1 crow (T).
- Cut 1 crow wing (U).

From assorted gold prints:
- Cut 1 small star (V).

Hugs and Kisses

From assorted blue prints:
- Cut 2 hugs (DD).
- Cut 4 kiss strips (EE).

Picket Fence and Sun Hat

From cream print:
- Cut 5 rectangles 2" x 7" for fence posts (FF).
- Cut 2 rectangles 1¹/₂" x 17" for fence rails (GG).

From assorted gold prints:
- Cut 1 sun hat brim (HH).
- Cut 1 sun hat top (KK).

From assorted blue prints:
- Cut 1 hat ribbon; cut 1 in reverse (II).
- Cut 1 hat center circle (JJ).

Butterfly Bush and Butterflies

From assorted green prints:
- Cut 3 stems; cut 2 in reverse (W).
- Cut 1 center of butterfly bush (X).
- Cut 1 left side of butterfly bush (Y).
- Cut 1 right side of butterfly bush (Z).

From assorted plum prints:
- Cut 5 butterfly bush flowers (AA).

From assorted gold prints:
- Cut 3 butterfly wings (BB).

From brown print scrap:
- Cut 3 butterfly bodies (CC).

ASSEMBLING THE BACKGROUND AND BORDERS

Follow **Piecing and Pressing,** *page 103. Refer to* **Quilt Assembly Diagram,** *page 31, for placement and use a ¹/₄" seam allowance.*

Background

1. Sew rectangles No. 2, 3, and 4 together to make Unit 1.
2. Sew rectangles No. 5, 6, 7, 8, 9 and 10 together to make Unit 2.
3. Sew rectangles No. 11 and 12 together; add rectangles No. 13, 14, and 15 to make Unit 3.
4. Sew rectangles No. 16 and 17 together to make Unit 4.
5. Sew Units 1, 2, 3 and Block 1 together to make Unit 5.
6. Sew Units 4, and 5 together to complete background.

Inner Border

1. Sew the top and bottom borders to the background.
2. Sew the side borders to the background.

Outer Border

1. Follow **Chain Piecing,** page 104, to sew the cream and blue triangles together to make 76 Triangle-Squares.

Triangle-Square (make 76)

2. Referring to **Quilt Assembly Diagram** for orientation, sew 16 Triangle-Squares together to make top outer border. Repeat to make bottom outer border.
3. Sew 22 Triangle-Squares together to make 1 side outer border. Repeat to make other side outer border.
4. Sew the top and bottom outer borders to the quilt top.
5. Sew the side outer borders to the quilt top.

ADDING THE APPLIQUÉ

*Refer to **Appliqué**, page 105, for techniques. Our quilt was appliquéd using the **Needleturn Appliqué** method. Refer to **Quilt Top Diagram**, page 32, and photo, page 28, for placement.*

Bias Tubing for Vines

Cut a 45" bias strip 1⅛"w from assorted green prints, piecing as necessary. With wrong sides together, fold strip in half lengthwise. Sew strip together ¼" from raw edges. Trim seam allowance to ⅛". Press tube with seam at center back. Cut 2 short honeysuckle vines 5½" long from finished tube, then use remaining tube for main stem. Appliqué the vines to the background, then add remaining appliqué pieces.

After completing the Honeysuckle Vine section, appliqué the remaining sections. Work in alphabetical order to position pieces, then pin or baste in place before appliquéing. Sew 8 black buttons on watermelon for seeds and 1 button on crow for an eye.

FINISHING

1. Follow **Quilting**, page 107, to mark, layer, and quilt as desired. Our quilt is machine quilted in the background with a vine pattern. Stars are added to the vine around the flags. Each appliqué shape is outline quilted. Veins are quilted in the center of each flower and a spiral design is quilted in the center of the hat. The border triangles are outline quilted.
2. Cut a 23" square of binding fabric. Follow **Binding**, page 110, to bind quilt using 2½"w bias binding with mitered corners.
3. Refer to **Making a Hanging Sleeve**, page 112, to make and attach a hanging sleeve.

Quilt Assembly Diagram

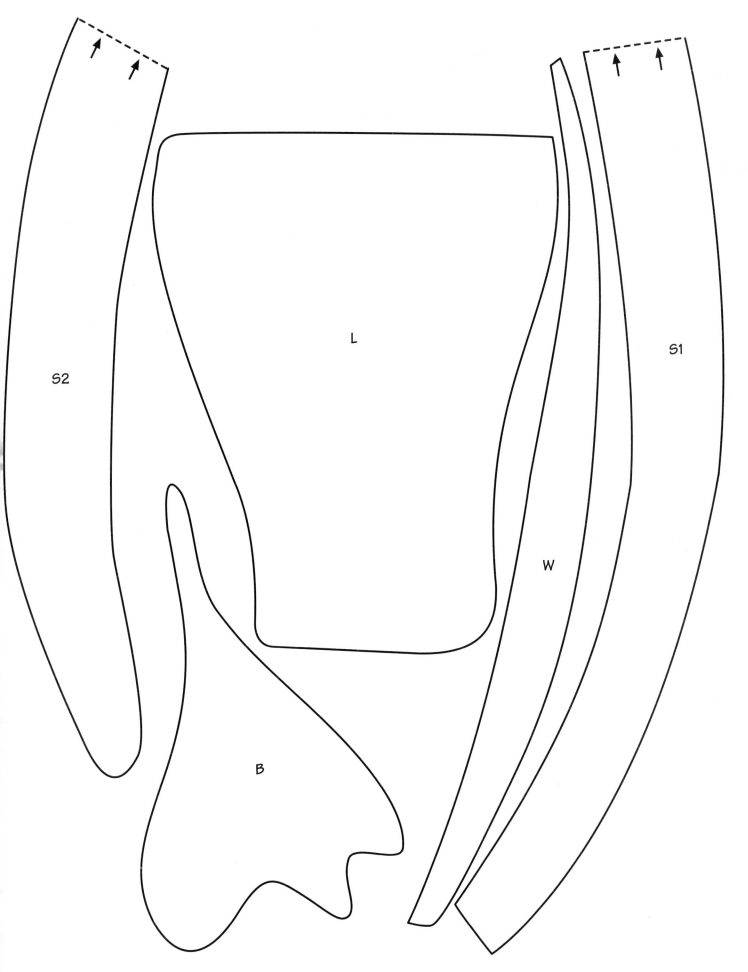

34

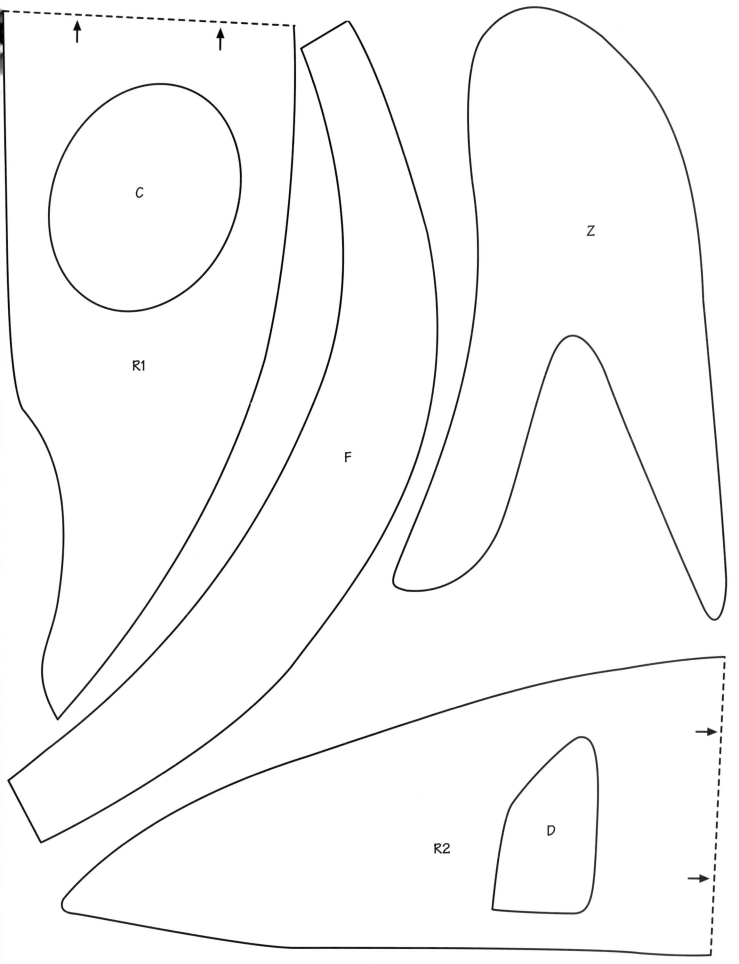

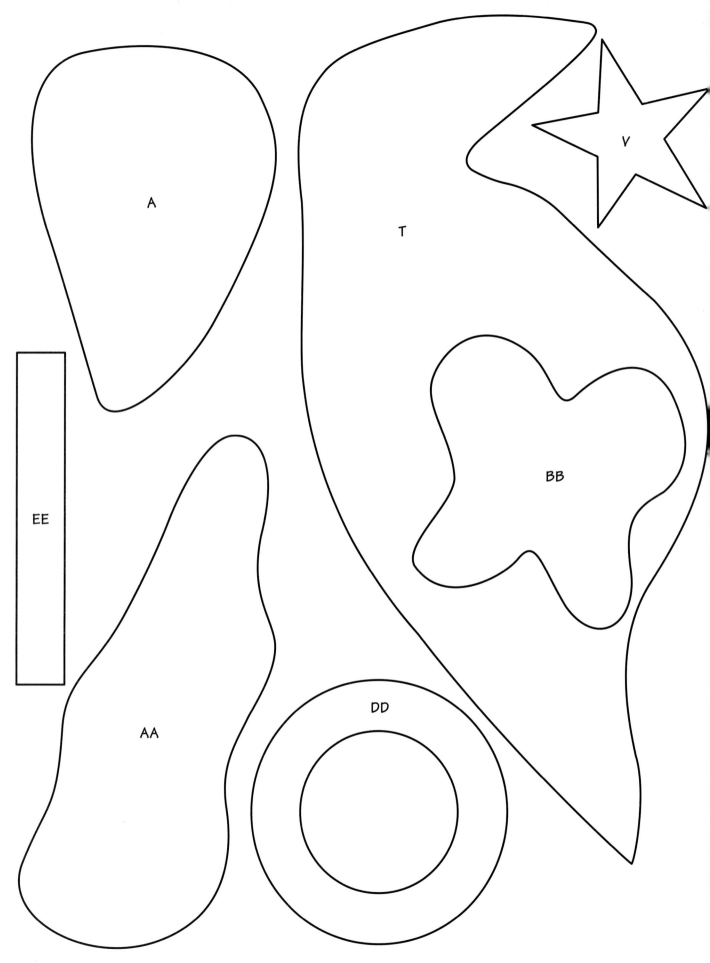

H

KK

HH

II

G

JJ

Ma-Ma's Garden

Take a trip back in time to Ma-Ma's garden — that memorable place where you spent your afternoons making daisy chains and chasing dragonflies. Country colors and free-form appliqués echo the innocence of a bygone era when life was simple and time slowed to a crawl.

FABRIC REQUIREMENTS

1 yd (91 cm) of assorted green prints
1/4 yd (23 cm) of assorted brown prints
1 yd (91 cm) of assorted cream and tan prints
1 1/4 yd (1.1 m) of assorted navy or black prints
1/2 yd (46 cm) of assorted blue prints
1/4 yd (23 cm) of assorted dark salmon prints
3/8 yd (34 cm) of assorted dark red prints
3/8 yd (34 cm) of assorted gold prints
3/4 yd (69 cm) of binding fabric
1 5/8 yds (1.5 m) of backing fabric
43" x 50" (109 x 127 cm) rectangle of batting

CUTTING THE BACKGROUND AND BORDERS

Yardage is based on 45"w fabric. Refer to **Rotary Cutting**, page 102, before beginning project. To help keep pieces organized, refer to **Quilt Assembly Diagram** to lay out the pieces as you cut.

From assorted green prints:
- Cut rectangle (No. 1) 7" x 8 1/2".
- Cut rectangle (No. 2) 1 1/2" x 8 1/2".
- Cut rectangle (No. 6) 4 1/2" x 13 1/2".
- Cut rectangle (No. 10) 18 1/2" x 10 1/2".
- Cut square (No. 12) 4 1/2" x 4 1/2".
- Cut square (No. 14) 4 1/2" x 4 1/2".
- Cut rectangle (No. 20) 12 1/2" x 2 1/2".

From assorted brown prints:
- Cut rectangle (No. 3) 3" x 8 1/2".
- Cut rectangle (No. 5) 6 1/2" x 1 1/2".
- Cut rectangle (No. 9) 1 1/2" x 27 1/2".
- Cut rectangle (No. 18) 1 1/2" x 8 1/2".

From assorted cream and tan prints:
- Cut rectangle (No. 4) 6 1/2" x 12 1/2".
- Cut rectangle (No. 7) 10 1/2" x 6 1/2".
- Cut rectangle (No. 8) 7 1/2" x 27 1/2".
- Cut rectangle (No. 15) 8 1/2" x 16 1/2".
- Cut rectangle (No. 16) 12 1/2" x 11 1/2".
- Cut rectangle (No. 17) 5 1/2" x 8 1/2".
- Cut rectangle (No. 19) 6 1/2" x 8 1/2".

From assorted navy or black prints:
- Cut square (No. 11) 4 1/2" x 4 1/2".
- Cut square (No. 13) 4 1/2" x 4 1/2".
- Cut rectangle (No. 21) 6 1/2" x 2 1/2".
- Cut rectangle (No. 22) 12 1/2" x 2 1/2".
- Cut rectangle (No. 24) 7 1/2" x 2 1/2".
- Cut rectangle (No. 25) 13 1/2" x 2 1/2".
- Cut rectangle (No. 26) 2 1/2" x 17 1/2".
- Cut rectangle (No. 27) 2 1/2" x 12 1/2".
- Cut rectangle (No. 29) 2 1/2" x 10 1/2".
- Cut rectangle (No. 31) 12 1/2" x 2 1/2".

- Cut rectangle (No. 33) 20 1/4" x 2 1/2".
- Cut rectangle (No. 34) 2 1/2" x 19 1/2".
- Cut rectangle (No. 35) 2 1/2" x 24 1/2".
- Cut rectangle (No. 36) 17 1/2" x 2 1/2".
- Cut rectangle (No. 38) 2 1/2" x 16 1/2".
- Cut rectangle (No. 40) 2 1/2" x 8 1/2".
- Cut 7 squares 2 7/8" x 2 7/8". Cut squares in half diagonally to make 14 triangles (you will use 13).

From assorted blue prints:
- Cut rectangle (No. 23) 6 1/2" x 2 1/2".
- Cut rectangle (No. 30) 2 1/2" x 17 1/2".
- Cut rectangle (No. 32) 2 3/4" x 2 1/2".
- Cut rectangle (No. 37) 19 1/2" x 2 1/2".
- Cut rectangle (No. 39) 2 1/2" x 21 1/2".
- Cut 3 squares 2 7/8" x 2 7/8". Cut squares in half diagonally to make 6 triangles (you will use 5).

From assorted dark salmon prints:
- Cut square (No. 28) 2 1/2" x 2 1/2".
- Cut 4 squares 2 7/8" x 2 7/8". Cut squares in half diagonally to make 8 triangles.

From assorted dark red prints:
- Cut 6 squares 2 7/8" x 2 7/8". Cut squares in half diagonally to make 12 triangles.

Quilt Assembly Diagram

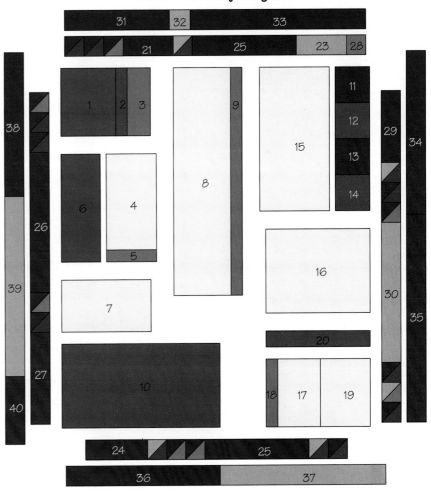

CUTTING THE APPLIQUÉS

Refer to **Making Templates**, page 104, to use patterns, pages 45-51, to make templates. **Note:** Appliqué patterns provided do not include seam allowances. Measurements given for rectangles include a ¼" seam allowance.

Coneflowers

From assorted blue prints:
- Cut 1 basket handle (A).
- Cut 1 basket (D).

From assorted green prints:
- Cut 1 stem; cut 1 in reverse (B).
- Cut 1 left stem (C).

From assorted dark salmon prints:
- Cut 1 heart (E).

From assorted dark red prints:
- Cut 15 petals (F).

From assorted navy or black prints:
- Cut 3 flower centers (G).

Black-eyed Susans

From assorted green prints:
- Cut 6 leaves (H).
- Cut 1 flower center (J).

From assorted gold prints:
- Cut 3 petals (I).

From assorted navy or black prints:
- Cut 1 flower center (J).

From assorted dark salmon prints:
- Cut 1 flower center (J).

Red Yarrow

From assorted blue prints:
- Cut 1 basket handle (K).
- Cut 1 basket (L).

From assorted green prints:
- Cut 1 left stem (M).
- Cut 1 center stem (N).
- Cut 1 right stem (O).

From assorted dark salmon prints:
- Cut 3 yarrow flowers (P).

From assorted dark red prints:
- Cut 5 yarrow flowers (P).

Hugs and Kisses

From assorted dark red prints:
- Cut 2 hugs (S).

From assorted dark salmon prints:
- Cut 4 kiss strips (T).

Lilies

From assorted navy or black prints:
- Cut 4 leaves; cut 2 in reverse (Q).

From assorted dark red prints:
- Cut 2 lily flowers (R).

Sunflower

From assorted green prints:
- Cut 1 stem (U1, U2, and U3).
- Cut 1 left leaf (V).
- Cut 1 right leaf (W).

From assorted brown prints:
- Cut 1 large flower center (X).

From assorted dark salmon prints:
- Cut 1 medium flower center (Y).
- Cut 1 small flower center (Z).

From assorted gold prints:
- Cut 11 petals (AA).

Bee Skep and Tulip

From assorted gold prints:
- Cut 1 bee skep handle (BB).
- Cut 1 bee skep (CC).
- Cut 1 bee skep door (DD).
- Cut 3 strips 1" x 9" (HH) for bees.

From assorted green prints:
- Cut 1 stem (EE1 and EE2).

From assorted dark salmon prints:
- Cut 1 tulip (FF).

From assorted cream and tan prints:
- Cut 3 bee wings; cut 3 in reverse (GG).

From assorted navy or black prints:
- Cut 3 strips 1" x 9" (HH) for bees.

Dragonfly

From assorted dark salmon prints:
- Cut 2 dragonfly upper wings (II).
- Cut 2 dragonfly lower wings (JJ).

From assorted brown prints:
- Cut 2 dragonfly bodies (KK).

ASSEMBLING THE BACKGROUND AND BORDERS

*Follow **Piecing and Pressing**, page 103. Refer to **Quilt Assembly Diagram**, page 41, for placement, and use a ¼" seam allowance.*

Background

1. Sew rectangles No. 1, 2, and 3 together to make Unit 1.
2. Sew rectangles No. 4 and 5 together; add rectangle No. 6, then No. 7 to make Unit 2.
3. Sew rectangles No. 8 and 9 together to make Unit 3.
4. Sew rectangles No. 11, 12, 13, and 14 together; add rectangle No. 15, then No. 16 to make Unit 4.
5. Sew rectangles No. 17, 18, and 19 together; add rectangle No. 20, then No. 10 to make Unit 5.
6. Sew Units together to complete the background.

Borders
Triangle Squares

Refer to **Chain Piecing**, page 104, to make triangle-squares in the following color combinations:

- Make 8 dark red and navy or black triangle-squares.
- Make 4 dark red and blue triangle-squares.
- Make 7 dark salmon and navy or black triangle-squares.
- Make 1 dark salmon and blue triangle-square.

Triangle-Square (make a total of 20)

Inner Border

Refer to **Quilt Assembly Diagram** for orientation of triangle-squares.

1. Sew 3 triangle-squares and rectangles No. 21, 22, and 23 together to make top inner border.
2. Sew 5 triangle-squares and rectangles No. 24 and 25 together to make bottom inner border.
3. Sew 6 triangle-squares and rectangles No. 26 and 27 together to make left side inner border.
4. Sew 6 triangle-squares, square No. 28, and rectangles No. 29 and 30 together to make right side inner border.
5. Sew top and bottom inner borders to background. Sew left and right inner borders to background.

Outer Border

1. Sew rectangles No. 31, 32, and 33 together to make top outer border.
2. Sew rectangles No. 34 and 35 together to make right side outer border.
3. Sew rectangles No. 36 and 37 together to make bottom outer border.
4. Sew rectangles No. 38, 39, and 40 together to make left side outer border.
5. Sew top outer border, then right side outer border to background. Sew bottom outer border, then left side outer border to background to complete quilt top.

ADDING THE APPLIQUÉ

Refer to **Needleturn Appliqué**, page 105, for technique. Refer to **Quilt Top Diagram** and photo, page 40, for placement. Appliqué pieces to background in alphabetical order. For bees, sew 5 HH's together to make a striped rectangle. Use bee body pattern (II) to cut 3 bodies; appliqué in place.

FINISHING

1. Follow **Quilting**, page 107, to mark, layer, and quilt as desired. Our quilt is hand quilted ¹/₂" from appliqués around the lilies, sunflower, tulip, bee skep, and coneflowers. The background and borders are quilted with large swirls and loops.

2. Cut a 23" square of binding fabric. Follow **Binding**, page 110, to bind quilt using 2¹/₂"w bias binding with mitered corners.

3. Refer to **Making a Hanging Sleeve**, page 112, to make and attach a hanging sleeve.

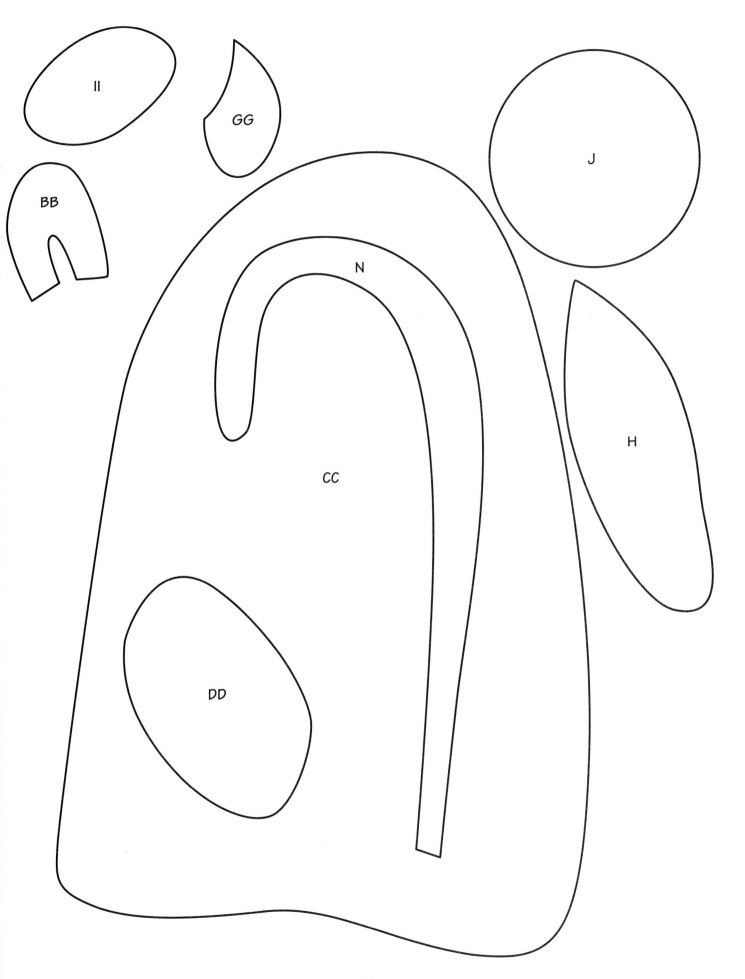

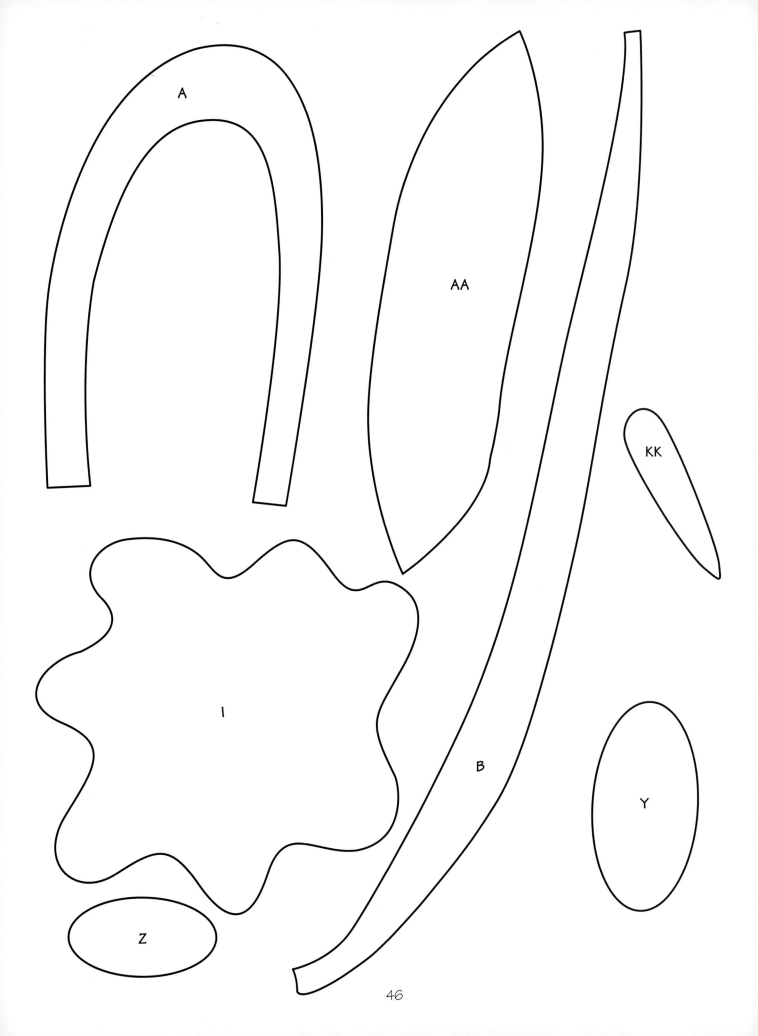

A

AA

KK

I

B

Y

Z

46

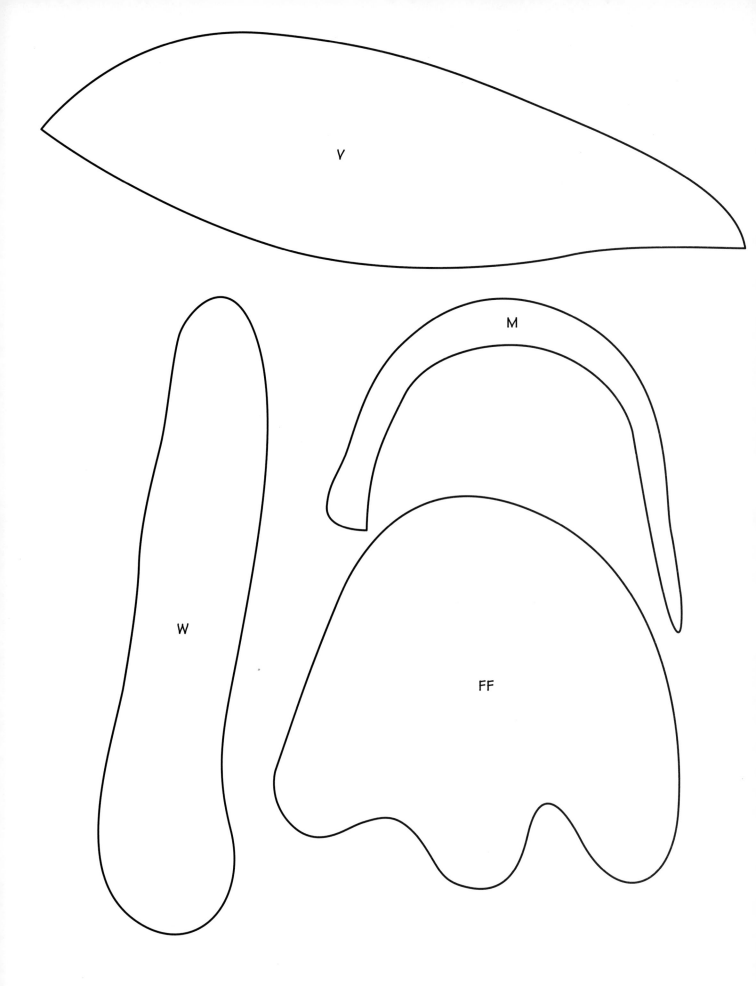

V

M

W

FF

K

R

X

Q

49

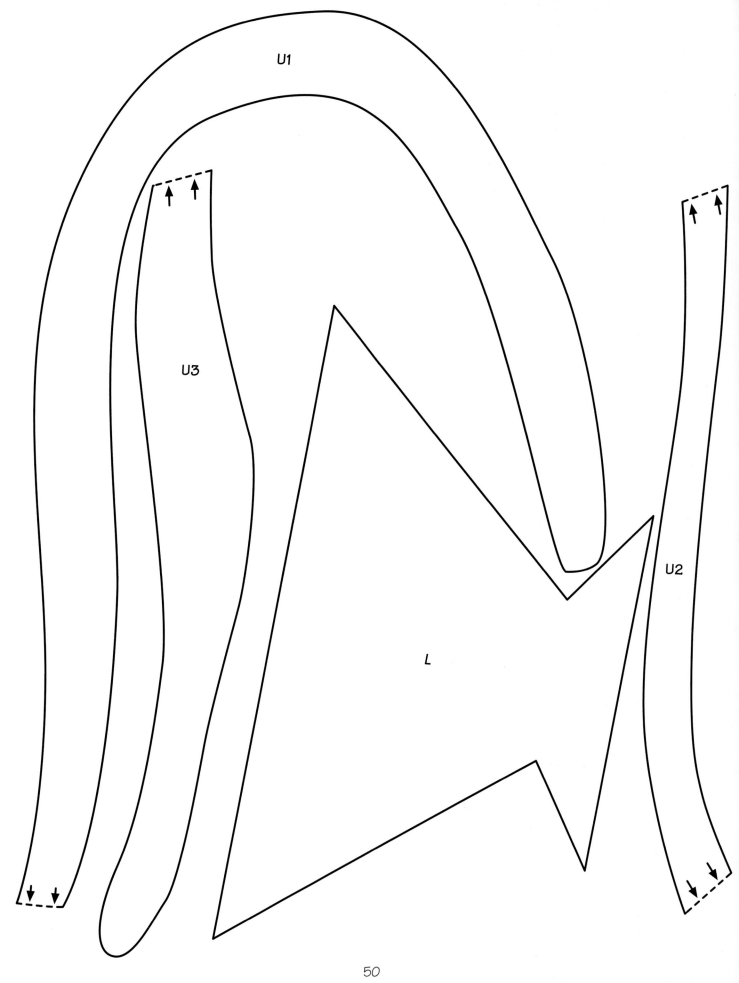

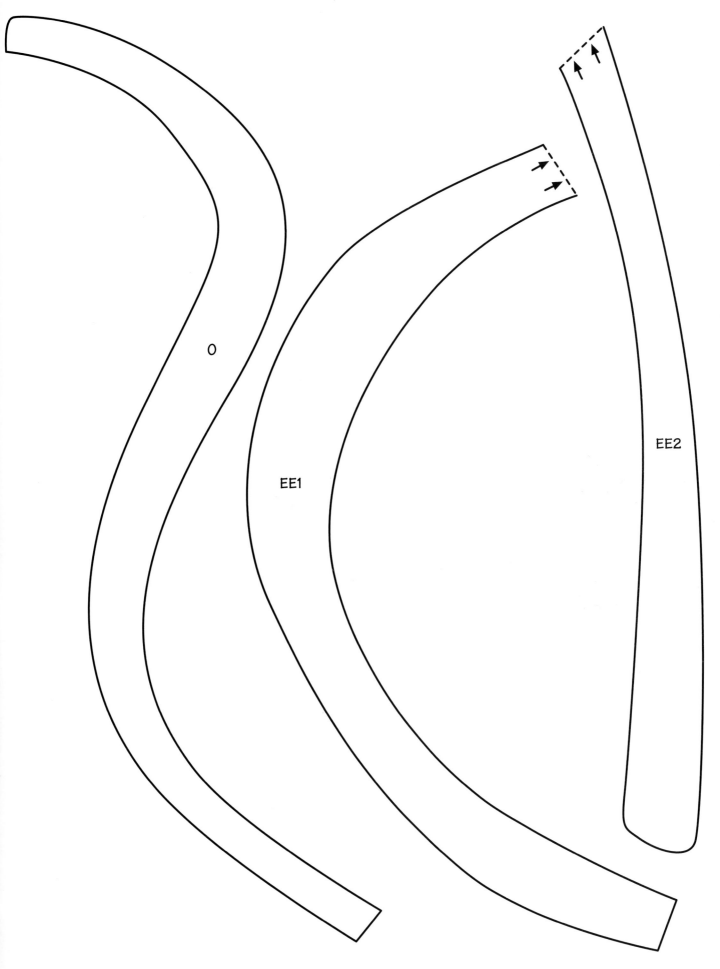

O

EE1

EE2

51

Harvest Moon

Surrounded by fall foliage and harvest's bounty, a sleek black cat preens quietly beneath a golden quarter-moon. A wide border sets off the scene, while a mixture of stripes and checks in muted golds and greens makes a captivating backdrop for this enchanted autumn eve.

HARVEST MOON
Finished Size: 38" x 38" (97 x 97 cm)

FABRIC REQUIREMENTS

1¼ yds (1.1 m) of assorted green plaids, stripes, and prints
¼ yd (23 m) of assorted tan plaids
¼ yd (23 cm) of cream plaid
⅞ yd (80 cm) of red floral print for inner border and binding
¾ yd (69 cm) of black stripe for outer border
¼ yd (23 cm) of orange plaid
½ yd (46 cm) of assorted gold prints
⅛ yd (11 cm) of navy print
¼ yd (23 cm) of black print
⅜ yd (34 cm) of red plaid
¼ yd (23 cm) of pumpkin print
¼ yd (23 cm) of pumpkin plaid
¼ yd (23 cm) of brown plaid
Scraps of assorted red prints for berries
1¼ yds (1.1 m) backing fabric
3 buttons (2 for the cat's eyes and 1 for the moon)
41" x 41" (104 x 104 cm) square of batting

CUTTING THE BACKGROUND AND BORDERS

Yardage is based on 45"w fabric. Refer to **Rotary Cutting**, page 102, before beginning project.

From cream plaid:
- Cut 4 squares 7⅞" x 7⅞". Cut each square once diagonally to make 8 triangles.

From assorted green plaids or stripes:
- Cut 16 squares 4" x 4".
- Cut 4 squares 7⅞" x 7⅞". Cut each square once diagonally to make 8 triangles.

From assorted tan plaids:
- Cut 16 squares 4" x 4".

From red floral print:
- Cut 2 strips 1½" x 28½" for inner top and bottom borders.
- Cut 2 strips 1½" x 30½" for inner side borders.

From black stripe:
- Cut 2 strips 4" x 30½" for outer top and bottom borders.
- Cut 2 strips 4" x 37½" for outer side borders.

CUTTING THE APPLIQUÉS

Refer to **Making Templates** and **Appliqué**, pages 104 and 105, to prepare and cut appliqué pieces. "Harvest Moon" was appliquéd using the **Needleturn Appliqué** method. All other appliqués were fused, then machine blanket-stitched.

From assorted gold prints:
- Cut 1 moon (A1 and A2).
- Cut 1 star (B).

From black print:
- Cut one black cat (C).

From black stripe:
- Cut 1 cat tail (D).

From orange plaid:
- Cut the letters "HARVEST MOON".

From navy print:
- Cut 1 basket opening (E).

From red plaid:
- Cut 1 basket handle (F).
- Cut 1 berry basket (G).

From assorted green prints:
- Cut 3 berry stems (H).
- Cut 1 right pumpkin vine (K1 and K2).
- Cut 1 Center Pumpkin Vine (L).
- Cut 1 left pumpkin vine (M).
- Cut 7 pumpkin leaves (O).

From red prints:
- Cut 21 berries (I).

From assorted green plaids:
- Cut 1 pumpkin stem (J).
- Cut 12 acorn leaves (P).

From pumpkin print:
- Cut 1 pumpkin (N).

From pumpkin plaid:
- Cut 8 acorns (Q).

From brown plaid:
- Cut 8 acorn caps (R).

ASSEMBLING THE QUILT TOP

1. Refer to **Piecing and Pressing**, page 103, to **Chain Piece** cream plaid and green stripe triangles to make 8 Triangle-Squares (**Unit 1**).

2. Sew 2 green and 2 tan squares together to make a Four Patch Block (**Unit 2**). Make 8 Unit 2's.

Unit 1 (make 8)   **Unit 2 (make 8)**

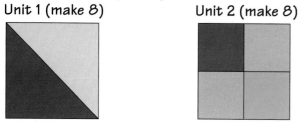

3. Referring to **Quilt Assembly Diagram** for placement, sew Unit 1's and 2's together.

4. Sew the top and bottom inner borders to the quilt top, then add the side inner borders. Sew the top and bottom outer borders to the quilt top, then add the side outer borders.

5. Refer to **Appliqué**, page 105, for techniques. Refer to **Quilt Top Diagram**, page 57, and photo, page 54, for placement. Working in alphabetical order, position pieces, then pin or baste in place before appliquéing.

FINISHING

1. Follow **Quilting**, page 107, to mark, layer, and quilt as desired. Our quilt is machine quilted with a meandering pattern in the background and outline quilting 1/4" from the inside edges of the moon, basket and cat. The pumpkin, leaves, and acorns have detail lines quilted on the appliqués to accent the shape.

2. Cut a 22" square of binding fabric. Follow **Binding**, page 110, to bind quilt using 2 1/2"w bias binding with mitered corners.

3. Refer to **Making a Hanging Sleeve**, page 112, to make and attach a hanging sleeve.

Quilt Assembly Diagram

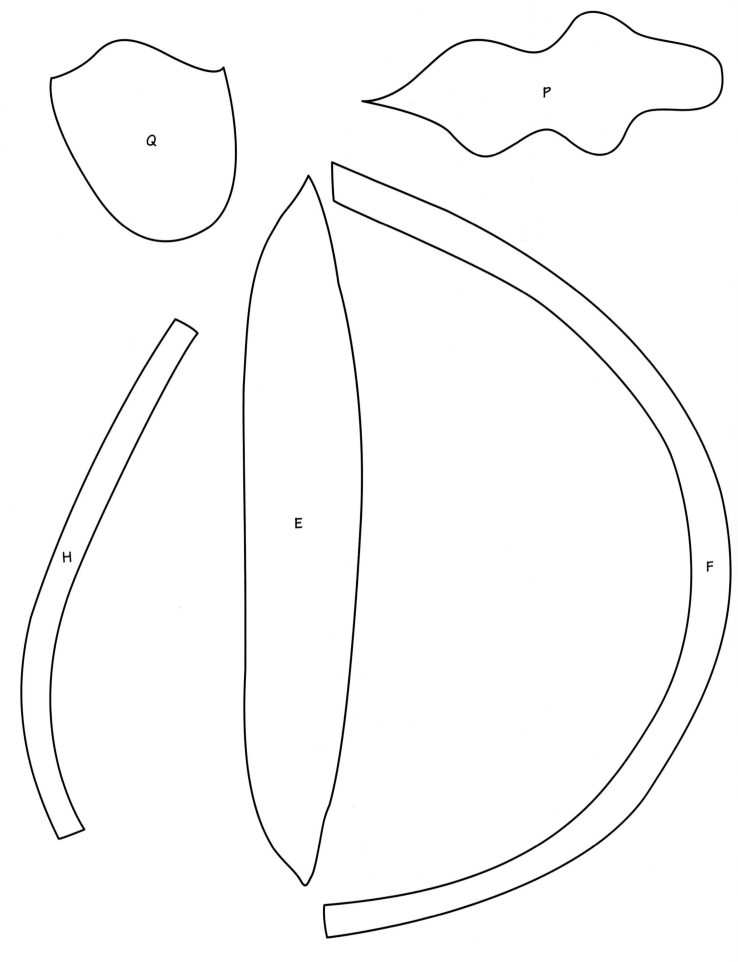

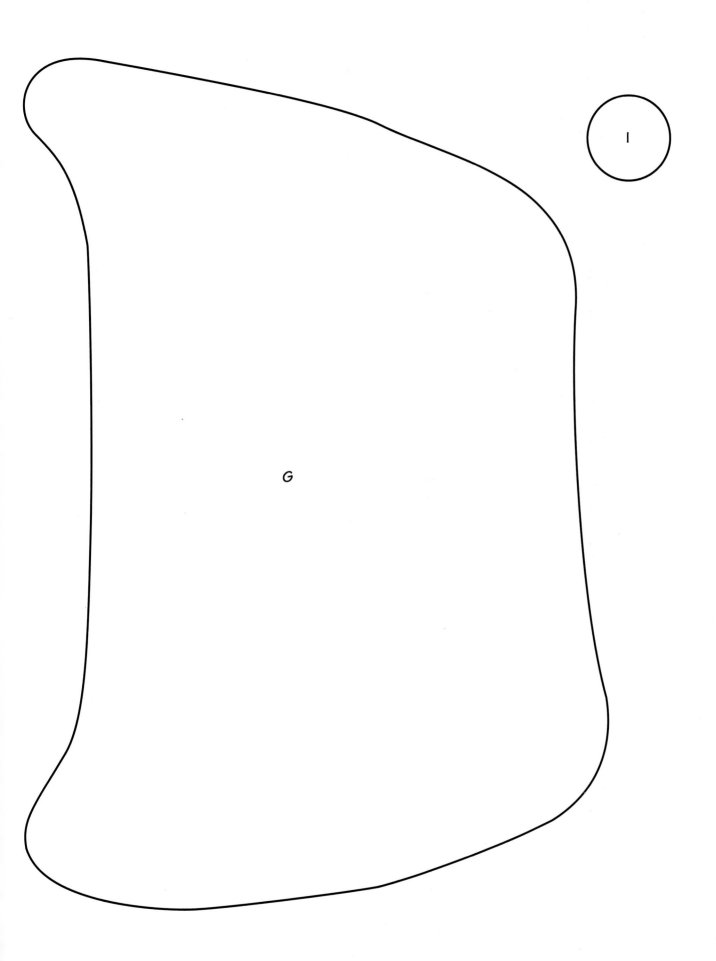

G

I

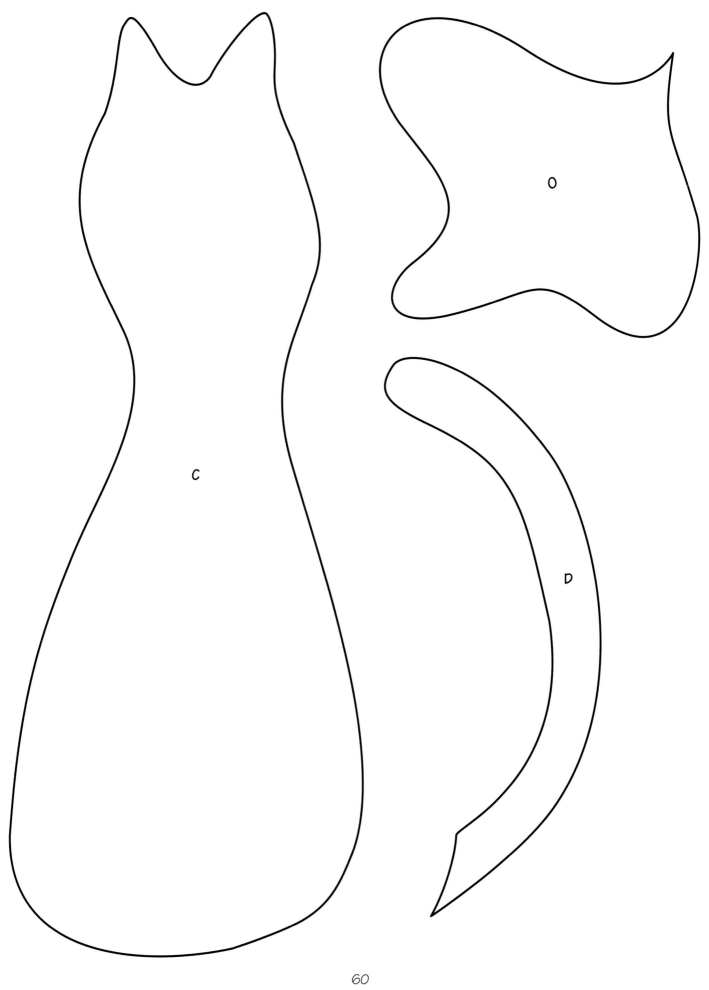

C

O

D

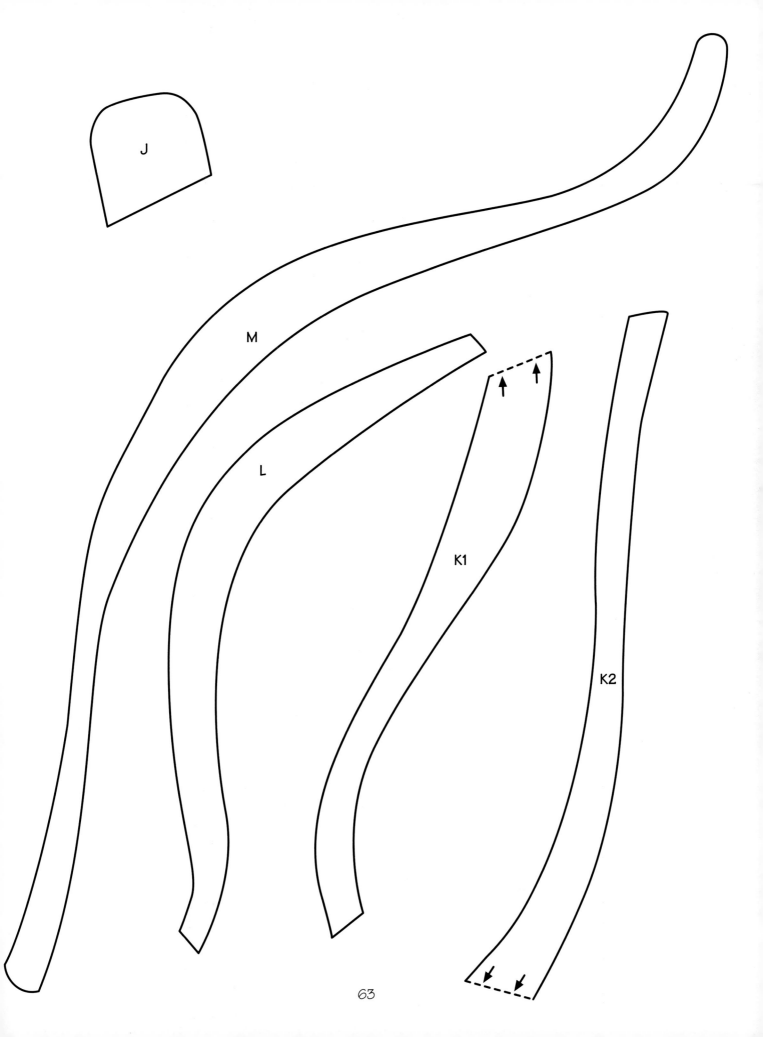

J

M

L

K1

K2

63

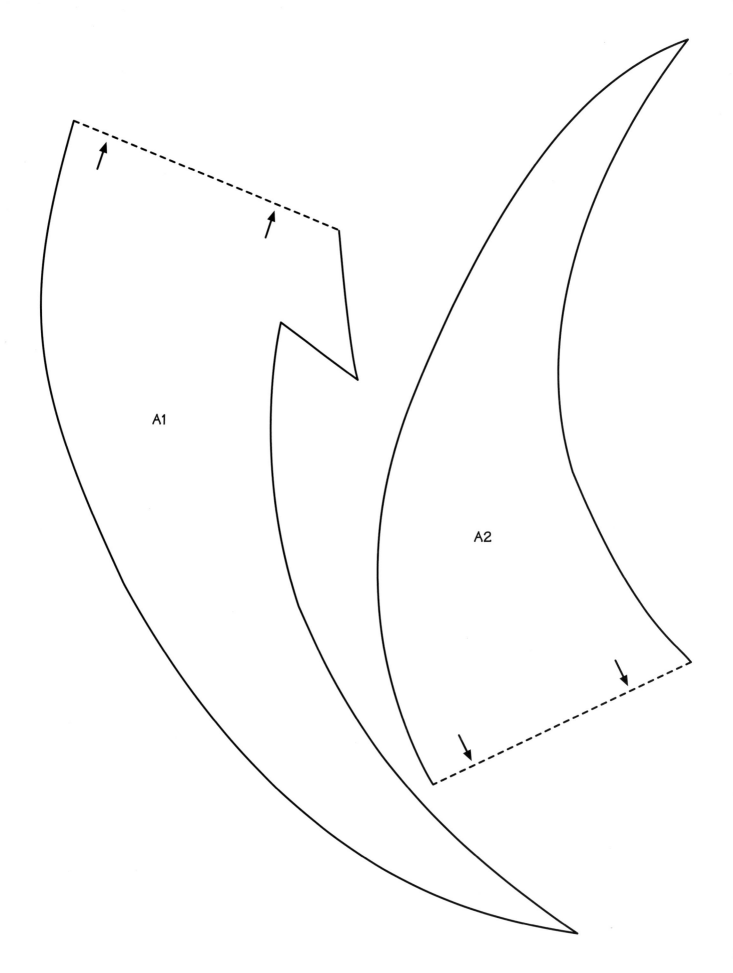

A1

A2

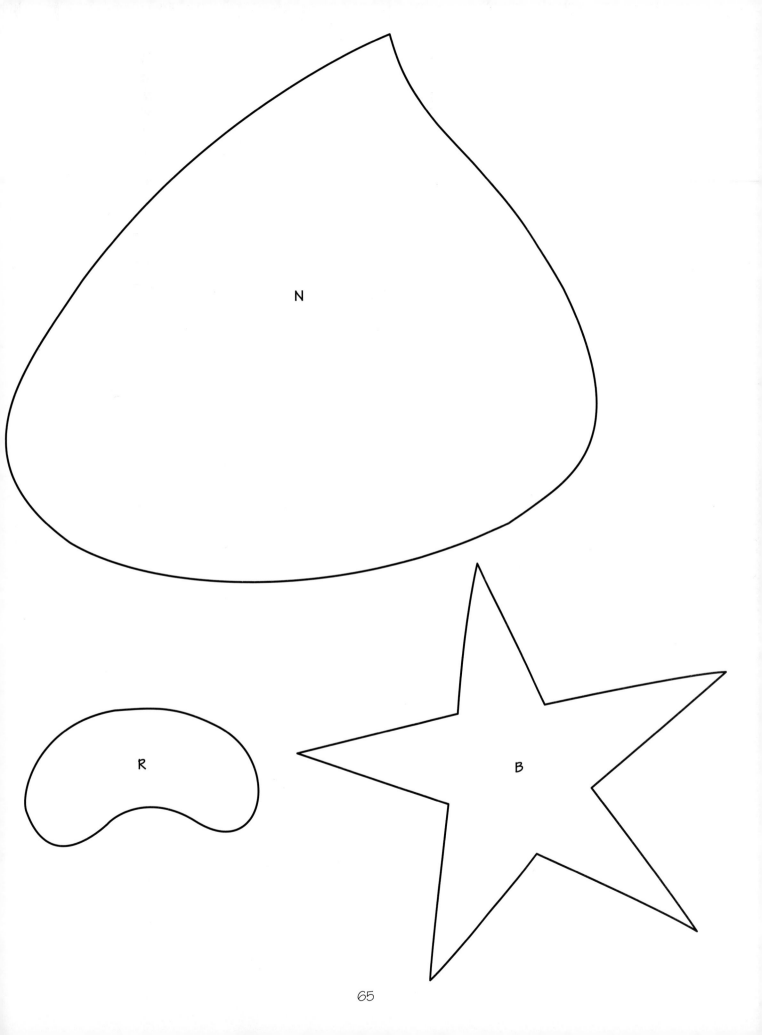

N

R

B

Basket of Hope

The night sky is alive with stars to wish upon, and cheerful posies nod in agreement as the gentle breeze whispers an assurance of good things to come. Patterned navy fabrics make the "sky" seem sparkly and vibrant, and a "dancing star" quilting pattern adds an air of hope.

BASKET OF HOPE
Finished Size: 68" x 68" (173 x 173 cm)

FABRIC REQUIREMENTS

3³/₈ yds (3.1 m) of navy print No. 1

1¹/₄ yds (1.1 m) of navy print No. 2

3 yds (2.7 m) of red plaid

¹/₂ yd (46 cm) of red print No. 1

¹/₄ yd (23 cm) of red print No. 2

¹/₄ yd (23 cm) of red floral print

¹/₄ yd (23 cm) of green polka dot

¹/₄ yd (23 cm) of green print

⁵/₈ yd (57 cm) of assorted gold prints

³/₄ yd (69 cm) of binding fabric

4 yds (3.7 m) of backing fabric

72" x 72" (183 x 183 cm) square of batting

CUTTING THE BACKGROUNDS AND BORDERS

Yardage is based on 45"w fabric. Refer to **Rotary Cutting**, page 102, before beginning project.

From navy print No. 1:
- Cut 2 lengthwise side outer borders 8¹/₂" x 68¹/₂".
- Cut 2 lengthwise top and bottom outer borders 8¹/₂" x 52¹/₂".
- Cut 8 large squares 8¹/₂" x 8¹/₂".
- Cut 10 squares 4⁷/₈" x 4⁷/₈". Cut squares in half diagonally to make 20 large triangles.
- Cut 11 medium squares 4¹/₂" x 4¹/₂".
- Cut 10 squares 2⁷/₈" x 2⁷/₈". Cut squares in half diagonally to make 20 small triangles.
- Cut 10 small squares 2¹/₂" x 2¹/₂".

From navy print No. 2:
- Cut 8 large squares 8¹/₂" x 8¹/₂".
- Cut 10 squares 4⁷/₈" x 4⁷/₈". Cut squares in half diagonally to make 20 large triangles.
- Cut 14 medium squares 4¹/₂" x 4¹/₂".
- Cut 10 squares 2⁷/₈" x 2⁷/₈". Cut squares in half diagonally to make 20 small triangles.
- Cut 10 small squares 2¹/₂" x 2¹/₂".

From red plaid:
- Cut 2 lengthwise side inner borders 2¹/₂" x 52¹/₂".
- Cut 2 lengthwise top and bottom inner borders 2¹/₂" x 48¹/₂".
- Cut 12 squares 4⁷/₈" x 4⁷/₈". Cut squares in half diagonally to make 24 large triangles.
- Cut 8 squares 2⁷/₈" x 2⁷/₈". Cut squares in half diagonally to make 16 small triangles.

From red print No. 1:
- Cut 8 squares 4⁷/₈" x 4⁷/₈". Cut squares in half diagonally to make 16 large triangles.
- Cut 12 squares 2⁷/₈" x 2⁷/₈". Cut squares in half diagonally to make 24 small triangles.

CUTTING THE APPLIQUÉS

Refer to **Making Templates** *and* **Fusible Appliqués**, *pages 104 and 105, to prepare and cut appliqué pieces. Our appliqués were fused then machine blanket-stitched.*

From assorted gold prints:
- Cut 17 small stars (E).
- Cut 12 large stars (I).

From red print No. 2:
- Cut 4 basket handles (A).
- Cut 16 dots (G).

From red floral:
- Cut 4 baskets (D).

From green polka dot:
- Cut 4 basket drapes (C).

From green print:
- Cut 12 strips 1" x 7" for stems (B).
- Cut 16 leaves (F).

From red plaid:
- Cut 12 swags (H) on fold.

MAKING THE BLOCKS

Refer to **Piecing and Pressing**, page 103, and **Fusible Appliqués,** page 105, to assemble the blocks.

Basket Block

1. Refer to **Basket Block Diagram** and photo for placement to make 4 Four-Patch blocks using 2 large squares each of navy print No. 1 and No. 2.
2. Work in alphabetical order to position pieces on background block before appliquéing.

Basket Block Diagram

Star-Within-A-Star Block

1. Refer to **Chain Piecing**, page 104, to piece the large and small triangles to make the following Triangle-Squares:
   - 8 small navy print No. 1 and red plaid Triangle-Squares.
   - 12 small navy print No. 1 and red print Triangle-Squares.
   - 8 small navy print No. 2 and red plaid Triangle-Squares.
   - 8 small navy print No. 2 and red print Triangle-Squares.
   - 12 large navy print No. 1 and red plaid Triangle-Squares.
   - 8 large navy print No. 1 and red print Triangle-Squares.
   - 12 large navy print No. 2 and red plaid Triangle-Squares.
   - 8 large navy print No. 2 and red print Triangle-Squares.

2. Referring to **Star Blocks Diagrams** for placement, use the Triangle-Squares and navy medium squares to make 3 Star Blocks 1 and 2 Star Blocks 2.

Star Block 1 Diagram (make 3)

Star Block 2 Diagram (make 2)

3. Appliqué a small star in the center of each Star Block.

ASSEMBLING THE QUILT TOP

1. Referring to the **Quilt Top Diagram**, page 71, and photo, page 68, for placement, sew the blocks together.
2. Sew the top and bottom inner borders to quilt top center, then the side inner borders.
3. Sew the top and bottom outer borders to the quilt top center, then the side outer borders.
4. Appliqué 3 swags (H) along each border; appliqué 1 star (I) over points where swags meet.

FINISHING

1. Follow **Quilting**, page 107, to mark, layer, and quilt as desired. Our quilt is machine outline-quilted around the baskets and stars. It is free-motion quilted with swirls and stars across the background and borders.
2. Cut a 29" square of binding fabric. Follow **Binding**, page 110, to bind quilt using 2¹/₂"w bias binding with mitered corners.

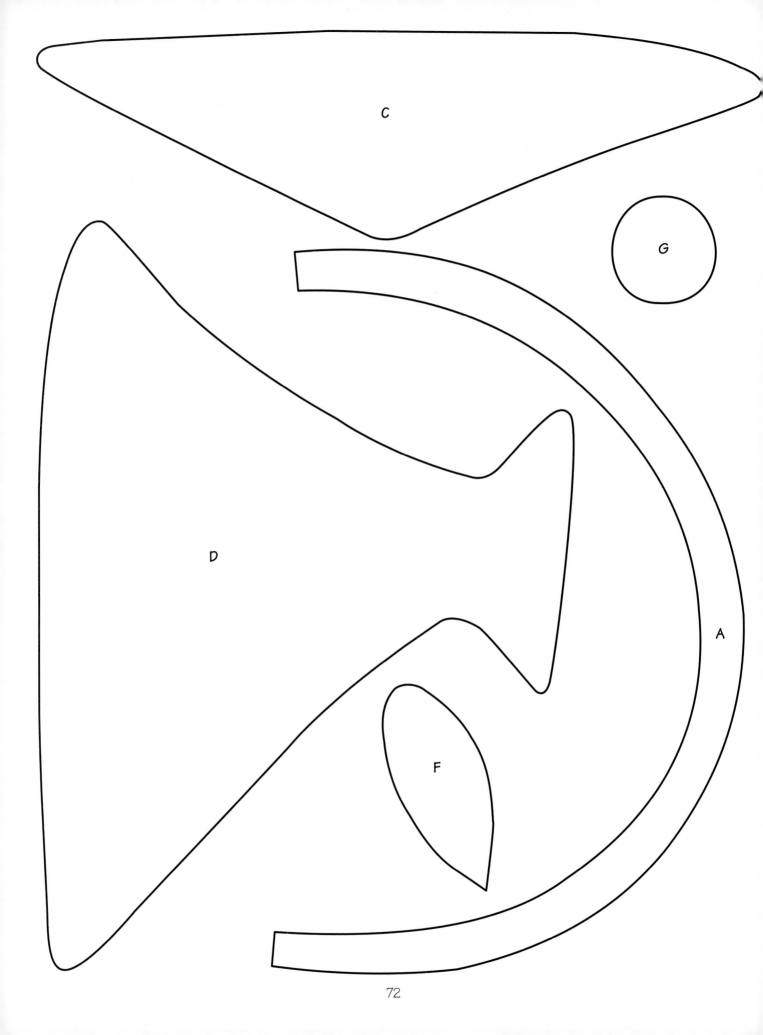

C

G

D

A

F

72

I

E

H

Fold

I Believe

Rustic reds and soft greens call to mind the cozy, close-knit feeling of Christmas, when you escape winter's chill by gathering 'round a toasty fire with family and friends. Decked out with everything from glorious poinsettias and peppermint candies to glittery snowflakes and sugarplum fairies, this jolly quilt is just right for celebrating the most magical time of year.

FABRIC REQUIREMENTS

2½ yds (2.2 m) of assorted cream and red prints
1 yd (91 cm) of assorted pale yellow prints
1⅝ yds (1.5 m) of assorted cream prints
½ yd (46 cm) of pale blue print
2⅝ yds (2.4 m) of assorted green prints
2 yds (1.8 m) of assorted red prints
⅝ yd (57 cm) assorted gold prints
⅛ yd (11 cm) white stripe
½ yd (46 cm) assorted brown prints
¼ yd (23 cm) assorted blue prints
⅜ yd (34 cm) assorted black prints and florals
½ yd (46 cm) black print for inner border
2¾ yds (2.5 m) red print for outer border
1 yd (91 cm) of binding fabric
5 yds (4.6 m) of backing fabric
75" x 93" (191 x 236 cm) batting

CUTTING THE BACKGROUNDS, SASHINGS, AND BORDERS

Yardage is based on 45"w fabric. Refer to **Rotary Cutting**, page 102, before beginning project. To help keep pieces organized, refer to the **Quilt Assembly Diagram** to lay out the pieces as you cut.

From assorted cream and red prints:
- Cut 3 rectangles (No. 1) 4½" x 12½".
- Cut 2 squares (No. 2) 12½" x 12½".
- Cut 1 rectangle (No. 6) 4½" x 20½".
- Cut 2 squares (No. 7) 8½" x 8½".
- Cut 2 rectangles (No. 8) 8½" x 4½".
- Cut 1 rectangle (No. 16) 8½" x 10½".
- Cut 1 rectangle (No. 18) 10½" x 13½".
- Cut 1 rectangle (No. 19) 6½" x 13½".
- Cut 1 rectangle (No. 20) 3½" x 7½".
- Cut 8 squares (No. 22) 5½" x 5½".
- Cut 1 rectangle (No. 23) 8½" x 16½".
- Cut 1 rectangle (No. 24) 8½" x 12½".

From assorted pale yellow prints:
- Cut 2 rectangles (No. 3) 9½" x 6½".
- Cut 1 rectangle (No. 4) 9½" x 2½".
- Cut 1 rectangle (No. 10) 7½" x 4½".
- Cut 1 rectangle (No. 11) 9½" x 4½".
- Cut 1 rectangle (No. 12) 16½" x 4½".
- Cut 4 squares (No. 13) 4½" x 4½".
- Cut 2 rectangles (No. 15) 20½" x "4½".

From assorted cream prints:
- Cut 1 rectangle (No. 5) 11½" x 14½".
- Cut 1 rectangle (No. 14) 6½" x 8½".
- Cut 1 square (No. 17) 12½" x 12½".
- Cut 1 rectangle (No. 21) 13½" x 7½".

From pale blue print:
- Cut 1 rectangle (No. 9) 16½" x 20½".

From assorted green prints:
- Cut 71 squares (No. 25) 2½" x 2½".
- Cut 105 squares 2⅞" x 2⅞". Cut squares in half diagonally to make 210 triangles.

From assorted red prints:
- Cut 23 squares (No. 26) 2½" x 2½".
- Cut 105 squares 2⅞" x 2⅞". Cut squares in half diagonally to make 210 triangles.

From black print for border:
- Cut 8 crosswise strips 1½"w.

From red print for border:
- Cut 2 lengthwise outer side borders 5½" x 84½".
- Cut 2 lengthwise outer top and bottom borders 5½" x 56½".

Quilt Assembly Diagram

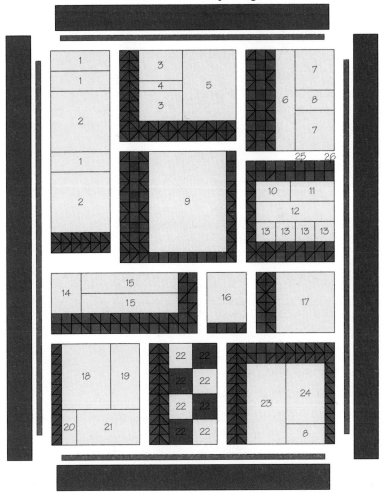

CUTTING THE APPLIQUÉS

*Refer to **Making Templates**, page 104, to use patterns, pages 84-99, to make templates. **Note:** Appliqué patterns provided do not include seam allowances. Measurements given for rectangles include a 1/4" seam allowance. To help keep blocks organized, lay out all appliqué pieces with corresponding backgrounds as you cut.*

Snowflakes

From assorted cream prints:
- Cut 6 of each snowflake piece (1a – 1g)
- Cut 3 snowflake centers (1h).

From assorted gold prints:
- Cut 3 stars (1i).

Sugarplum Faeries

From white stripe:
- Cut 1 wing (2a).
- Cut 1 wing (2b).
- Cut 1 wing (2c).

From assorted black prints:
- Cut 6 feet (2d).
- Cut 1 dress (2f).

From assorted green prints:
- Cut 1 slip (2e).
- Cut 2 dresses (2f).

From assorted gold prints:
- Cut 2 slips (2e).

From assorted cream prints:
- Cut 3 faces (2g).

From assorted brown prints:
- Cut 3 hair shapes (2h).

From assorted red prints:
- Cut 4 sugarplums (2i).
- Cut 3 sugarplum hearts (2j).

From assorted cream and red prints:
- Cut 3 sugarplums (2i).
- Cut 4 sugarplum hearts (2j).

Feed the Birds

From assorted black prints:
- Cut 1 birdhouse (3a).
- Cut 1 cardinal face (3n).

From assorted pale yellow prints:
- Cut 1 birdhouse door (3b).

From assorted blue prints:
- Cut 1 birdhouse roof (3c).
- Cut 1 birdhouse loop (3d).

From assorted cream prints:
- Cut 1 birdhouse snow (3e).
- Cut 1 top branch snow (3g).
- Cut 1 bottom branch snow (3h).

From assorted brown prints:
- Cut 1 branch (3f).

From assorted green prints:
- Cut 1 bird feeder stand (3i).
- Cut 1 bird feeder bowl (3j).
- Cut 1 bird feeder (3l).

From assorted gold prints:
- Cut 1 birdseed (3k).

From assorted red prints:
- Cut 1 cardinal (3m).

Granny's House and Pappy's Shed

From assorted cream prints:
- Cut 1 snow bank (4a). (To make template for snow bank, cut 16" x 3 1/2" rectangle from paper and attach to bottom of snow bank template. Add seam allowances.)

From assorted red prints:
- Cut 1 rectangle 7 1/8" x 8 1/4" for house front (4b).
- Cut 1 house side (4c).
- Cut 1 shed front (4f).
- Cut 1 shed side (4g).

From assorted black prints:
- Cut 2 rectangles 2" x 1 1/2" for chimneys (4d).
- Cut 1 house roof (4e).
- Cut 1 shed roof (4h).
- Cut 1 wreath left bow loop (4p).
- Cut 1 wreath right bow loop (4q).
- Cut 1 wreath bow tail; cut 1 in reverse (4r).
- Cut 1 wreath bow knot (4s)

From assorted gold prints:
- Cut 1 rectangle 4" x 1 3/4" for house door (4i).
- Cut 1 rectangle 3" x 1 3/4" for shed door (4j).
- Cut 7 rectangles 1 1/2" x 2" for house windows (4k).
- Cut 2 rectangles 1 1/2" x 1 1/4" for shed windows (4l).
- Cut 1 rectangle 2" x 1 1/4" for side house window (4m).
- Cut 3 stars (1i).

From assorted brown prints:
- Cut 1 tree (4n1 and 4n2).

From assorted green prints:
- Cut 1 wreath (4o).

From assorted blue prints:
- Cut 2 swirls (4t).

I Believe—Hugs and Kisses

From assorted green prints:
- Cut 1 each of the letters "I Believe".
- Cut 2 hugs (5a).
- Cut 4 rectangles 1" x 3 3/4" for kisses.

From assorted black prints:
- Cut 1 large heart (5c).

From assorted red prints:
- Cut 1 small heart (5d).

A Crow in the Bittersweet and Holly

From assorted brown prints:
- Cut 1 left branch (6a1 and 6a2).
- Cut 1 right branch (6b).

From assorted gold prints:
- Cut 9 bittersweet shapes (6c).

From assorted red prints:
- Cut 9 bittersweet centers (6d).
- Cut 3 holly berries (6f).

From assorted green prints:
- Cut 9 holly leaves (6e).

From assorted black prints:
- Cut 1 crow (6g).

Candy Cone

From assorted red prints:
- Cut 2 candy canes; cut 1 in reverse (7a).
- Cut 1 heart (7g).
- Cut 12 peppermint swirls (7i).

From assorted green prints:
- Cut 1 left stem (7c).
- Cut 1 right stem (7d).
- Cut 1 bias strip 1" x 8" for middle stem (7e).

From assorted black prints:
- Cut 1 cone handle (7b).
- Cut 1 cone (7f).

From white stripe:
- Cut 3 peppermints (7h).

From assorted gold prints:
- Cut 4 stars (1i).

Cookie Jar

From assorted red prints:
- Cut 1 jar base (8a).
- Cut 1 cookie jar on fold (8b).
- Cut 1 lid (8d).

From assorted gold prints:
- Cut 1 lid knob (8e).

From assorted brown prints:
- Cut 1 spoon (8f).

From assorted green prints:
- Cut 1 neck ribbon (8c).
- Cut 1 left bow tail (8g).
- Cut 1 right bow tail (8h).
- Cut 1 left bow loop (8i).
- Cut 1 right bow loop (8j).
- Cut 1 bow knot (8k).

Oh Christmas Tree

From assorted gold prints:
- Cut 1 rectangle $1^3/4$" x 16" for tree trunk (9a).
- Cut 1 star (1i).

From assorted green prints:
- Cut 1 rectangle $1^1/2$" x $12^1/2$ for branch (9b).
- Cut 1 rectangle $1^1/2$" x $11^1/2$ for branch (9c).
- Cut 1 rectangle $1^1/2$" x $9^1/2$ for branch (9d).
- Cut 1 rectangle $1^1/2$" x 8 for branch (9e).
- Cut 1 rectangle $1^1/2$" x $5^1/2$ for branch (9f).
- Cut 1 rectangle $1^1/2$" x $4^1/2$ for branch (9g).
- Cut 1 tree pot (9h).

From assorted red prints:
- Cut 12 berries (9i).

The Stockings Were Hung

From assorted red prints:
- Cut 2 stockings (10a1 and 10a2).

From assorted cream prints:
- Cut 2 cuffs (10b).
- Cut 2 heels (10c).
- Cut 2 toes (10d).

Poinsettia Blooms

From assorted green prints:
- Cut 1 rectangle $1^1/2$" x $3^1/2$ for stem (11a).
- Cut 1 rectangle $1^1/2$" x 8 for stem (11b).
- Cut 1 rectangle $1^1/2$" x 4 for stem (11c).
- Cut 8 leaves (11g).

From assorted black prints:
- Cut 1 flowerpot (11d).
- Cut 1 rectangle $1^1/2$" x $8^1/2$" for flowerpot rim (11e).

From assorted gold prints:
- Cut 1 large star (11f).
- Cut 3 flower centers (11j).

From assorted red prints:
- Cut 3 flower backgrounds (11h).
- Cut 12 petals (11i).

MAKING THE BLOCKS

*Refer to **Needleturn Appliqué**, page 105, for technique. Refer to the **Block Diagrams** and photo, page 76, for placement. **Note:** Some of the appliqués on this quilt extend beyond the edges of their background blocks onto the sashing strips and borders. The sashing strips and borders may be sewn to background blocks before appliquéing, or the appliqué edges that extend may be left unstitched (pin edges out of the way) until the sashing strips and borders are attached.*

Triangle-Squares for Sashings

1. Refer to **Piecing and Pressing**, page 103, to **Chain Piece** green triangles and red triangles together to make 210 Triangle-Squares (**Unit 1**).

Unit 1 (make 210)

2. Sew 2 Unit 1's together to make 62 Flying Geese Blocks (**Unit 2**).

Unit 2 (make 62)

3. Sew 4 Unit 1's, 4 (No. 25) green squares, and 1 (No. 26) red square together to make 6 Shoofly Blocks (**Unit 3**).

Unit 3 (make 6)

Snowflakes

1. Sew background pieces No. 1 and 2 together.
2. Refer to the **Block Diagram** and photo, page 76, for placement of appliqué pieces. Work in alphabetical order to position pieces, then pin or baste in place before appliquéing.
3. Sew 6 Unit 2's together to make the bottom Sashing Strip. Sew strip to bottom edge of block.

Snowflakes Block Diagram

Sugarplum Faeries

1. Sew background pieces No. 3, 4, and 5 together.
2. Refer to the **Block Diagram** and photo, page 76, for placement of appliqué pieces. Work in alphabetical order to position pieces, then pin or baste in place before appliquéing.
3. Sew 7 Unit 2's together to make the left Sashing Strip. Sew strip to left edge of block. Sew 12 Unit 2's together to make the bottom Sashing Strip. Sew strip to bottom edge of block.

Sugarplum Faeries Block Diagram

Feed the Birds

1. Sew background pieces No. 7, 8, and 6 together.
2. Refer to the **Block Diagram** and photo, page 76, for placement of appliqué pieces. Work in alphabetical order to position pieces, then pin or baste in place before appliquéing.

3. Sew 3 Unit 3's, 2 Unit 2's and 1 green square together to make the left Sashing Strip. Sew strip to left edge of block.

Feed the Birds Block Diagram

Granny's House and Pappy's Shed

1. Appliqué top edge of 4a onto background No. 9. Bottom and side edges will be sewn into the seams later.

2. Refer to the **Block Diagram** and photo, page 76, for placement of appliqué pieces. Work in alphabetical order to position pieces, then pin or baste in place before appliquéing.

3. Sew 4 red and 4 green squares together to make the bottom Sashing Strip. Sew strip to bottom edge of block.

4. Sew 4 Unit 3's, 2 green, and 1 red square together to make the right Sashing Strip. Sew strip to right edge of block.

5. Sew 3 Unit 3's and 3 Unit 2's together to make the left Sashing strip. Sew strip to left edge of block.

Granny's House and Pappy's Shed Block Diagram

I Believe—Hugs and Kisses

1. Sew background pieces No. 10, 11, 12, and 13 together.

2. Refer to the **Block Diagram** and photo, page 76, for placement of appliqué pieces. Work in alphabetical order to position pieces, then pin or baste in place before appliquéing.

3. Sew 3 Unit 3's together to make the left Sashing strip. Sew strip to left edge of block.

4. Sew 3 Unit 3's, 6 green squares and 6 Unit 1's together to make the bottom Sashing strip. Sew strip to bottom edge of block.

5. Sew 2 Unit 2's, 9 green squares, and 7 red squares together to make the top Sashing strip. Sew strip to top edge of block.

I Believe—Hugs and Kisses Block Diagram

A Crow in the Bittersweet and Holly

1. Sew background pieces No. 14 and 15 together.

2. Refer to the **Block Diagram** and photo, page 76, for placement of appliqué pieces. Work in alphabetical order to position pieces, then pin or baste in place before appliquéing.

3. Sew 4 Unit 1's and 4 green squares together to make the right Sashing Strip. Sew strip to right edge of background.

4. Sew 14 Unit 1's, 15 green squares and 1 red square together to make the bottom Sashing Strip. Sew strip to bottom edge of block.

A Crow in the Bittersweet and Holly Block Diagram

Candy Cone

1. Refer to the **Block Diagram** and photo, page 76, for placement of appliqué pieces. Work in alphabetical order to position pieces, then pin or baste in place before appliquéing.

2. Sew 1 Unit 1, 1 green square, and 2 red squares together to make the bottom Sashing Strip. Sew strip to bottom edge of block.

Candy Cone Block Diagram

Cookie Jar

1. Refer to the **Block Diagram** and photo, page 76, for placement of appliqué pieces. Work in alphabetical order to position pieces, then pin or baste in place before appliquéing.
2. Sew 4 Unit 2's, 2 green squares, 1 red square and 1 Unit 1 together to make left Sashing Strip. Sew strip to left edge of block.

Cookie Jar Block Diagram

Oh Christmas Tree

1. Sew background pieces No. 18, 19, 20, and 21 together.
2. Refer to the **Block Diagram** and photo, page 76, for placement of appliqué pieces. Work in alphabetical order to position pieces, then pin or baste in place before appliquéing.
3. Sew 10 Unit 1's together to make left Sashing Strip. Sew strip to left edge of block.

Oh Christmas Tree Block Diagram

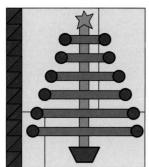

The Stockings Were Hung

1. Sew 8 background squares No. 22 together.
2. Refer to the **Block Diagram** and photo, page 76, for placement of appliqué pieces. Work in alphabetical order to position pieces, then pin or baste in place before appliquéing.
3. Sew 10 Unit 2's together to make left Sashing Strip. Sew strip to left side of block.

The Stockings Were Hung Block Diagram

Poinsettia Blooms

1. Sew background pieces No. 8, 23, and 24 together.
2. Refer to the **Block Diagram** and photo, page 76, for placement of appliqué pieces. Work in alphabetical order to position pieces, then pin or baste in place before appliquéing.
3. Sew 8 Unit 1's together to make right Sashing Strip. Sew strip to right side of block.
4. Sew 6 Unit 2's, 2 Unit 1's and 3 green squares together to make top Sashing Strip. Sew strip to top edge of block.
5. Sew 8 Unit 2's together to make left Sashing Strip. Sew strip to left side of block.

Poinsettia Blooms Block Diagram

ASSEMBLING THE QUILT TOP

Referring to the **Quilt Assembly Diagram**, page 77, for placement, sew the blocks together.

1. Sew the Sugar Plum Faeries and Granny's House blocks together; add the Snowflakes Block to make Unit 1.

2. Sew the Feed the Birds and I Believe blocks together to make Unit 2.

3. Sew the Crow in the Bittersweet and Holly, Candy Cone and Cookie Jar blocks together to make Unit 3.

4. Sew the Christmas Tree, Stockings, and Poinsettia blocks together to make Unit 4.

5. Sew Units 1 and 2 together; add Unit 3, then Unit 4 to complete the quilt top center.

ADDING THE BORDERS

1. Sew 2 strips together to make the top, bottom, left side, and right side inner borders.

2. Sew the top and bottom inner borders to the quilt top, then add the side borders.

3. Sew the top and bottom outer borders to the quilt top, then add the side borders.

4. Finish appliquéing all pieces that extend into the border to complete the quilt top.

FINISHING

1. Follow **Quilting**, page 107, to mark, layer, and quilt as desired. Our quilt is machine quilted with stipple quilting in backgrounds, green squares and green halves of Triangle-Squares. Detail quilting is added to larger appliqué pieces such as the roof of the house, the cookie jar, and the sugarplum faerie dresses. The outer border is quilted with a bow pattern.

2. Cut a 30" square of binding fabric. Follow **Binding**, page 110, to bind quilt using 2¹⁄₂"w bias binding with mitered corners.

Quilt Top Diagram

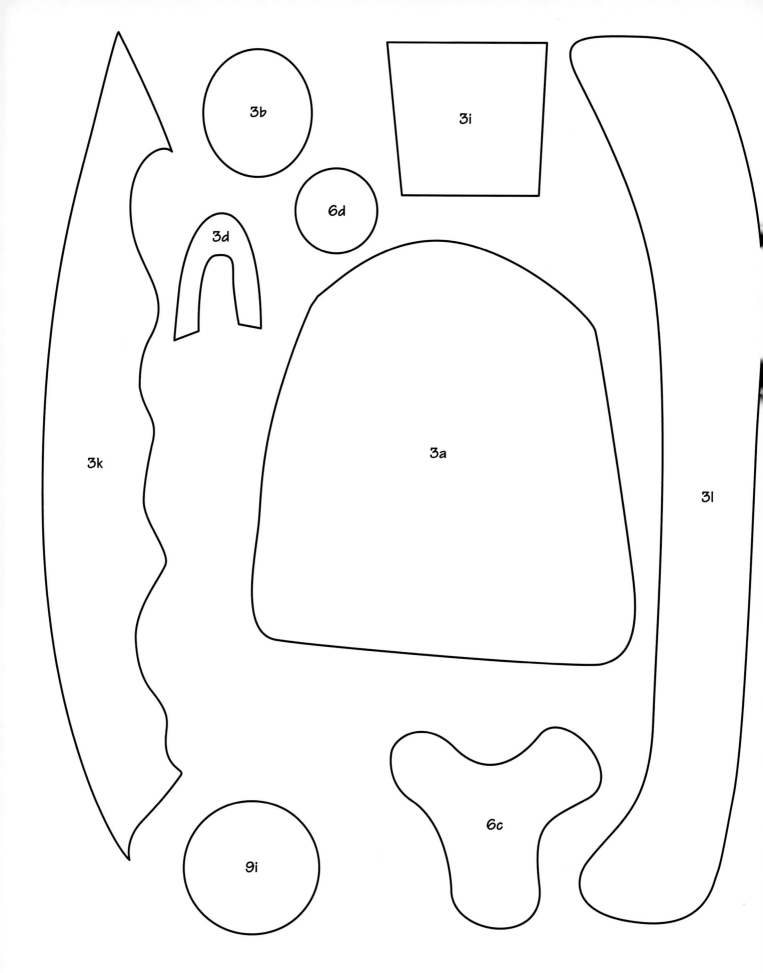

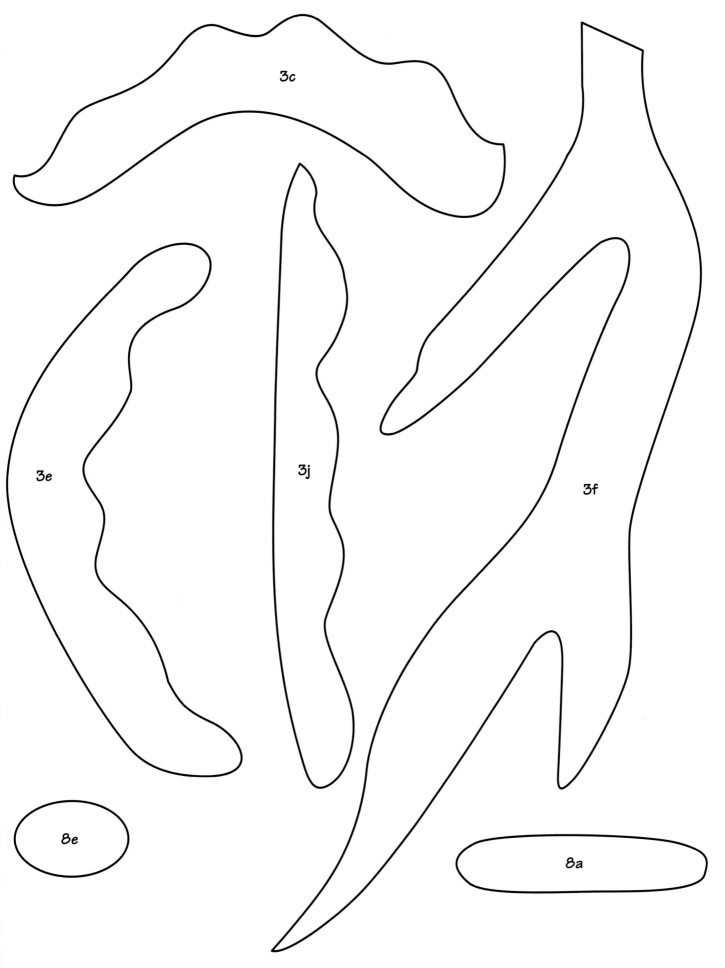

1f

1g

7a

4r

8k

3n

8h

8i

7g

8d

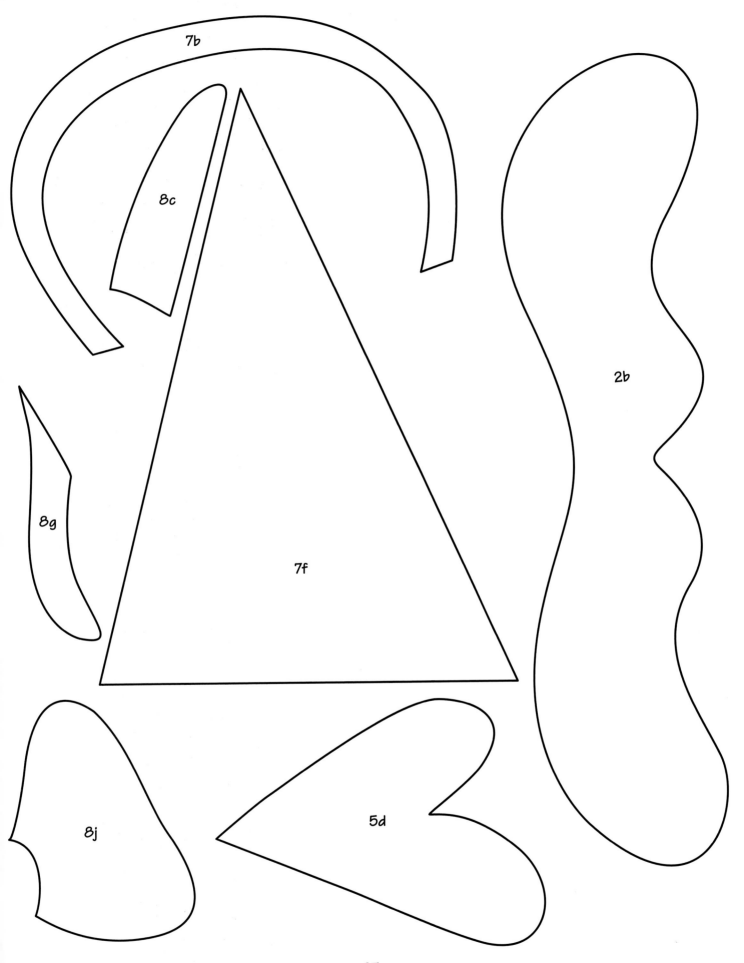

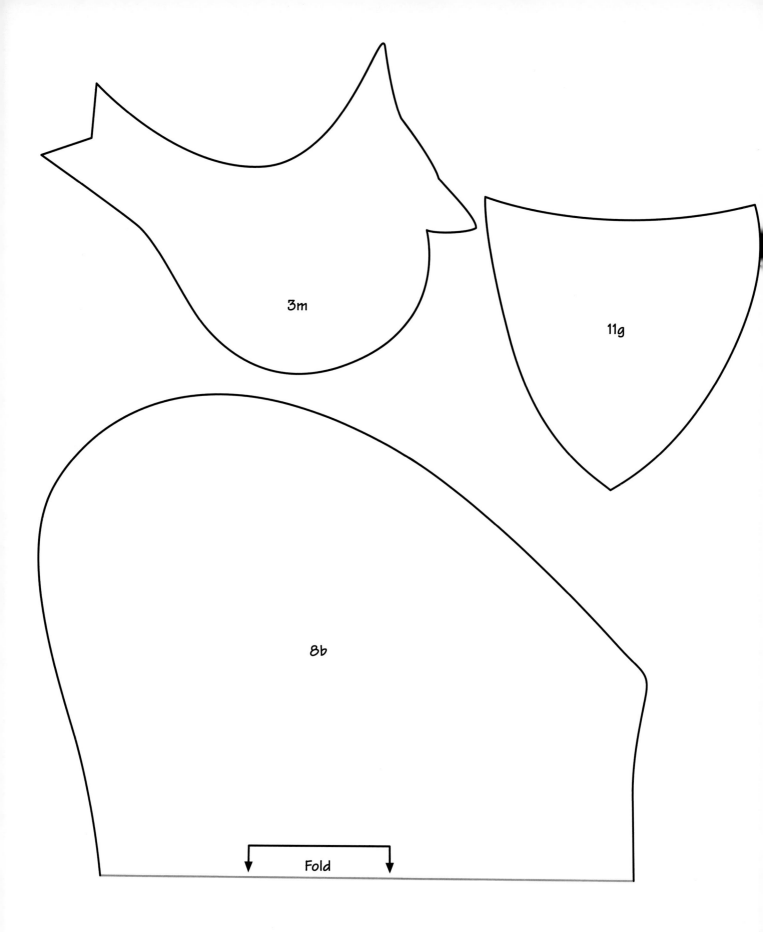

3m

11g

8b

Fold

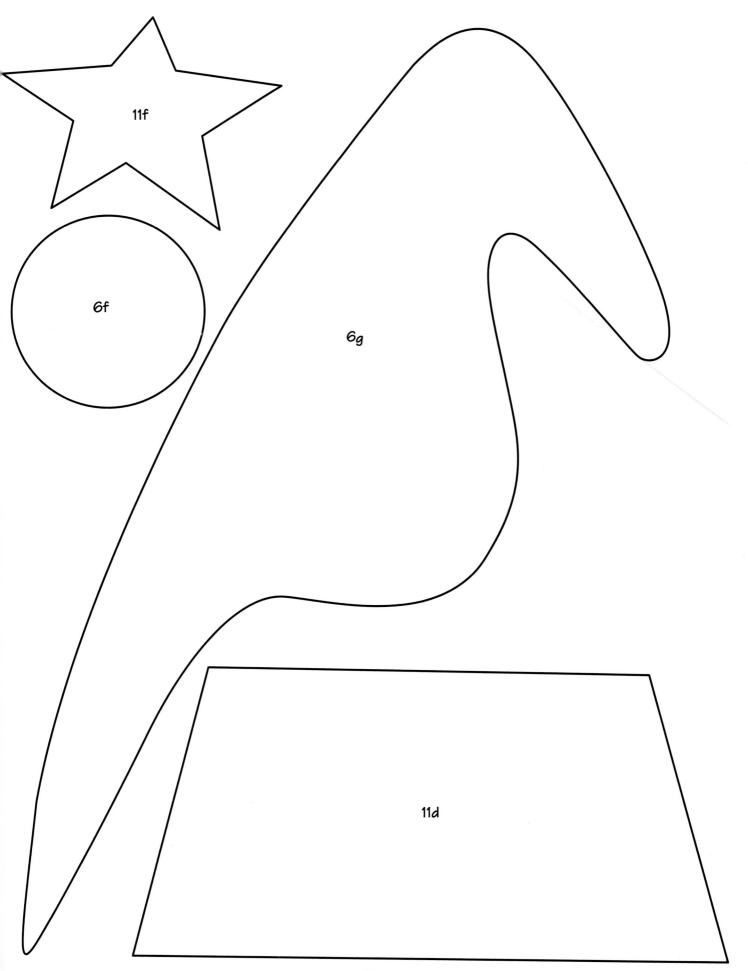

11f

6f

6g

11d

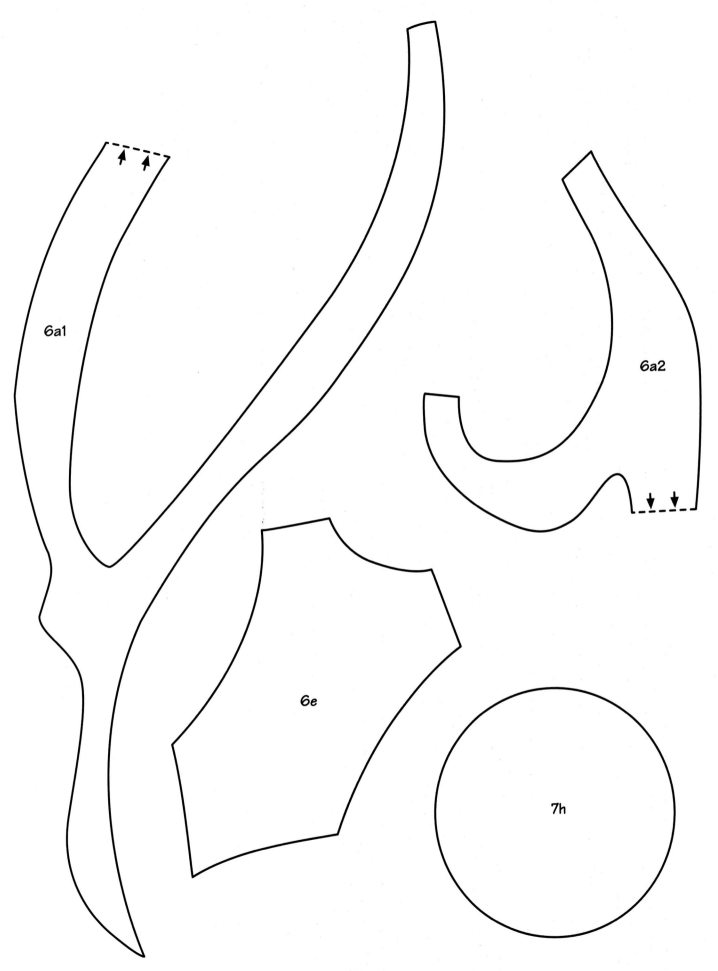

6a1

6a2

6e

7h

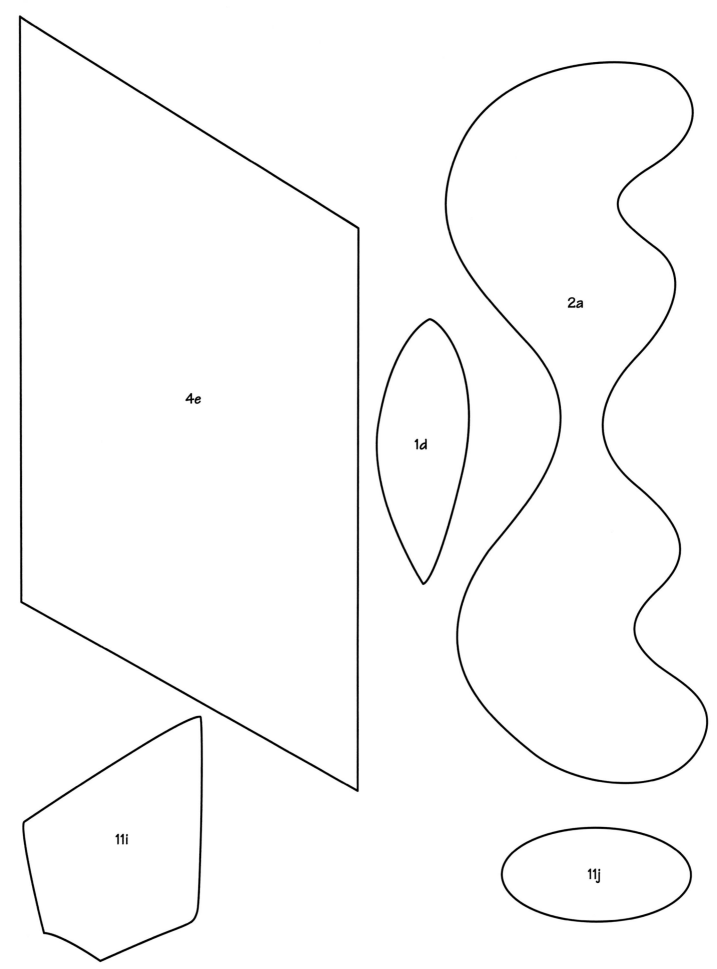

4e

2a

1d

11i

11j

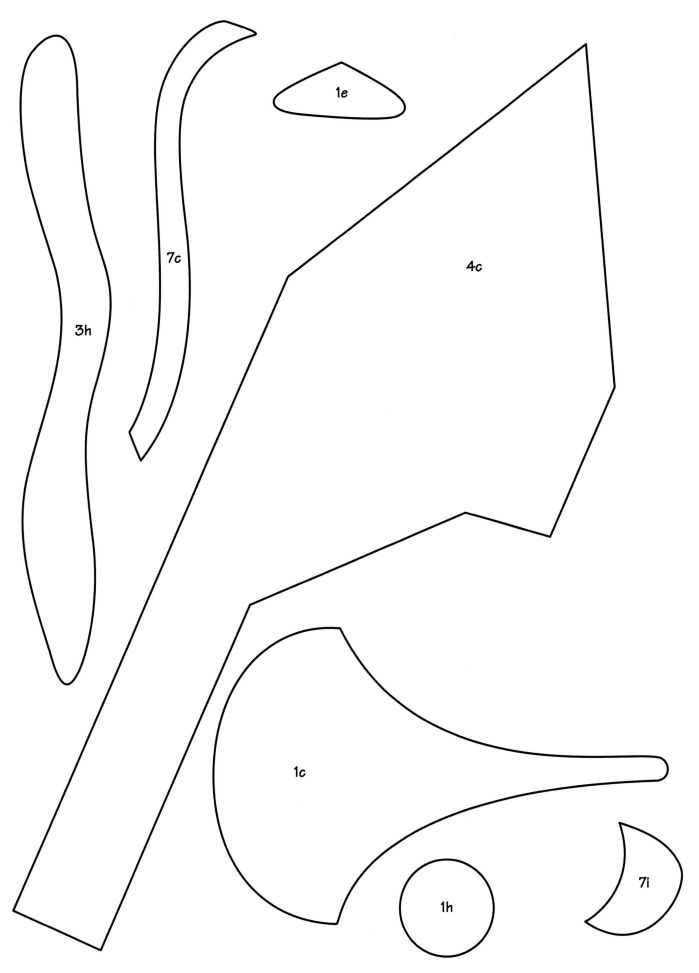

5a

4a

4h

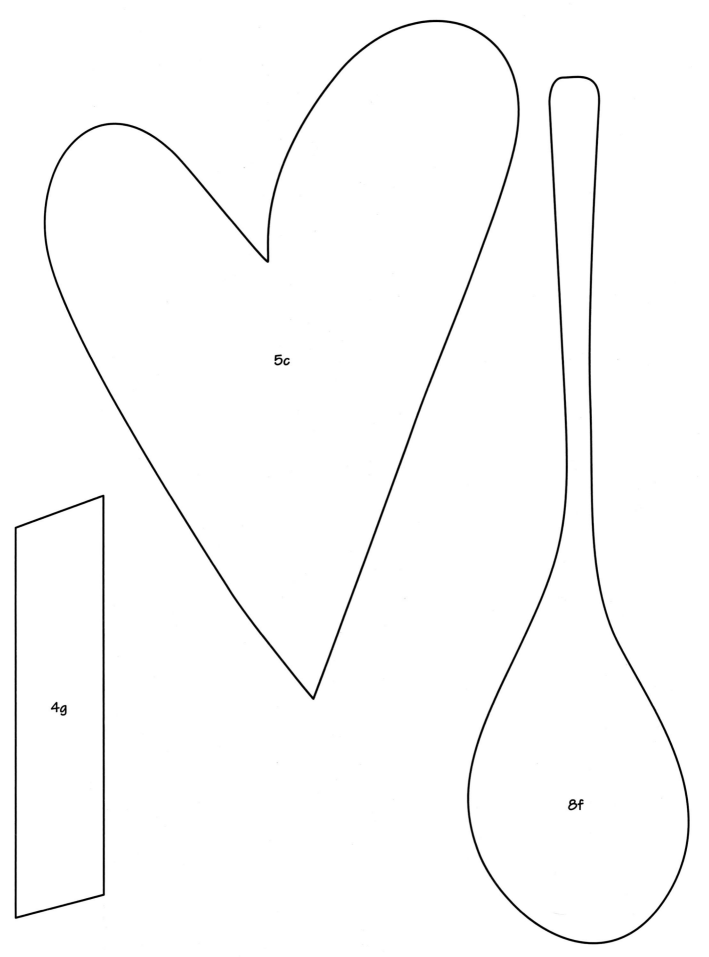

5c

4g

8f

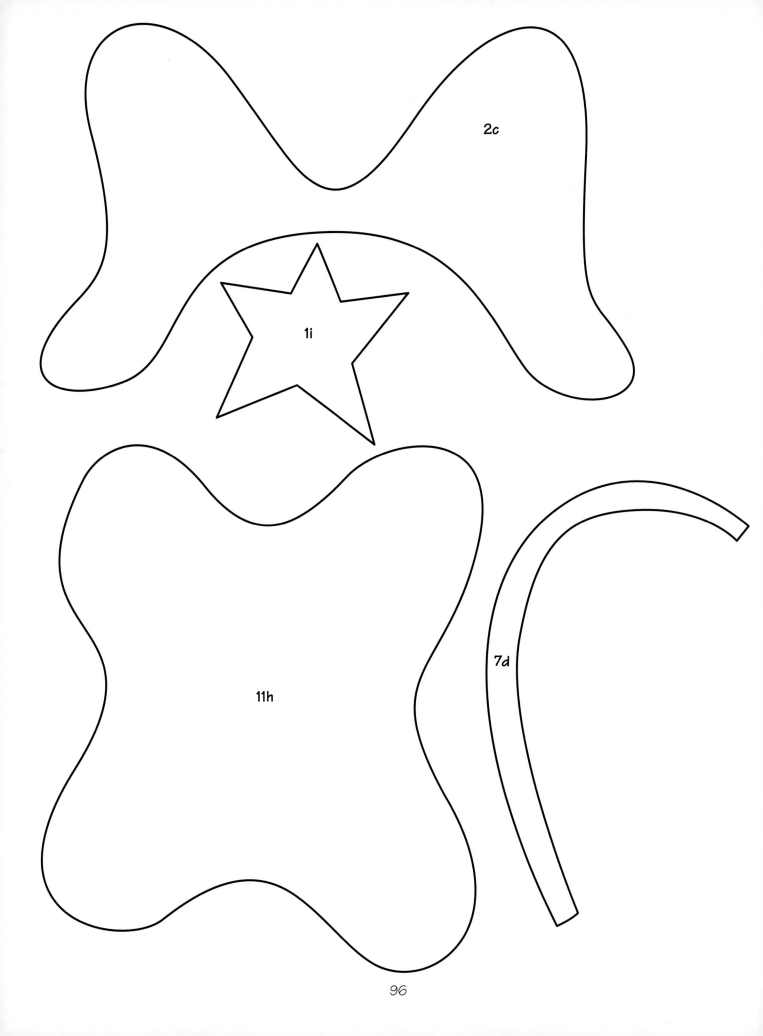

2c

1i

11h

7d

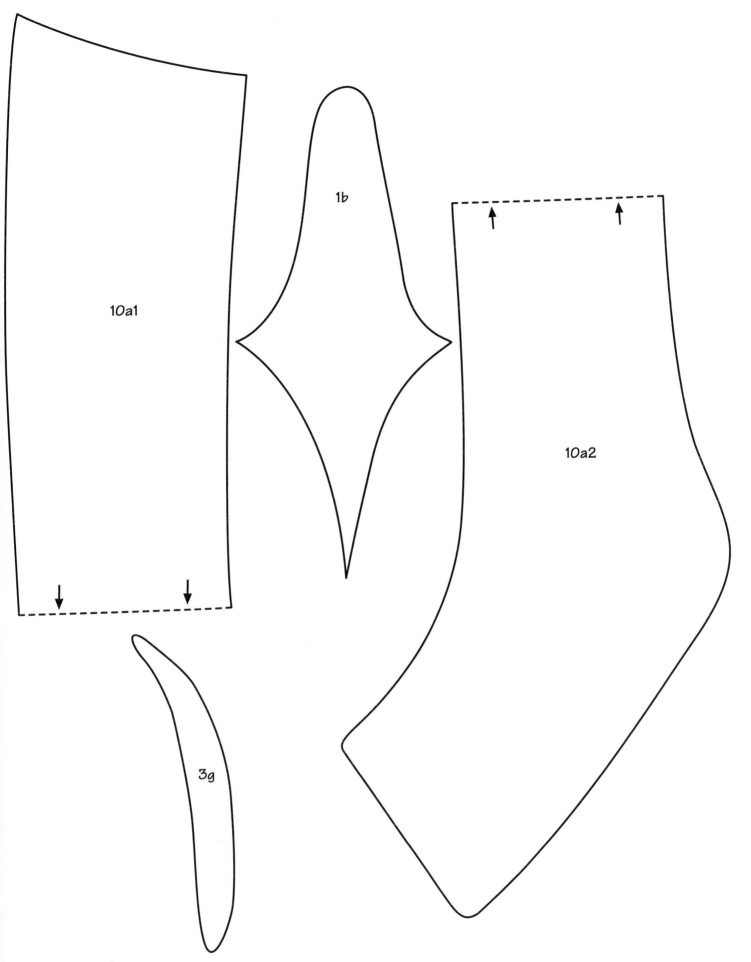

10a1

1b

10a2

3g

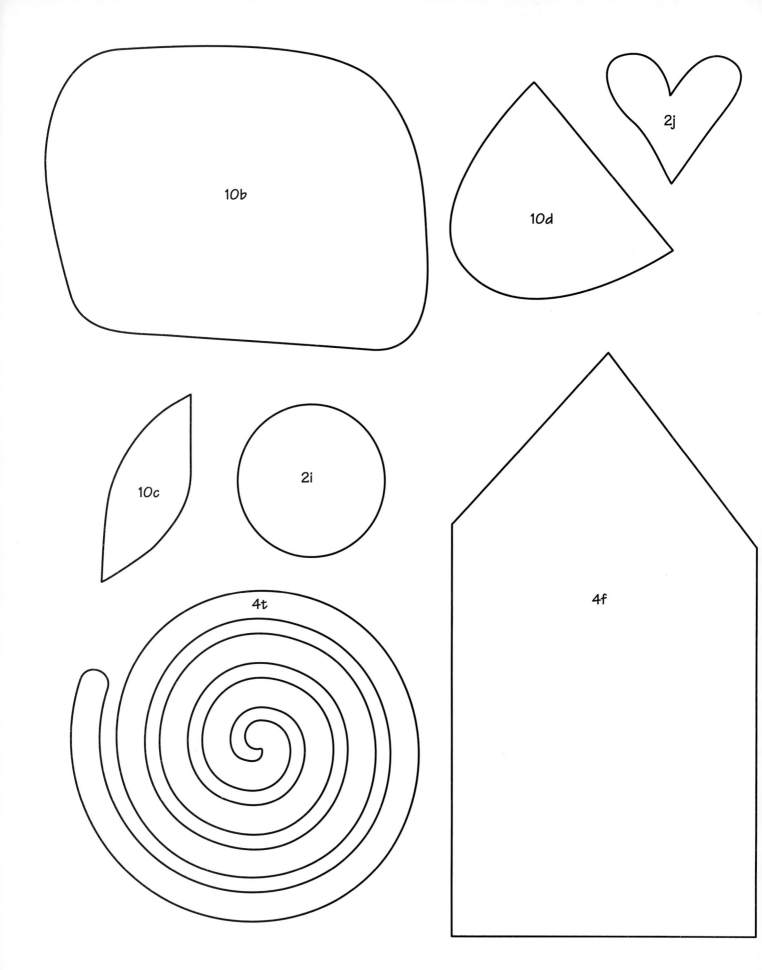

10b

2j

10d

10c

2i

4t

4f

GENERAL INSTRUCTIONS

Complete instructions are given for making each of the quilts shown in this book.
To make your quilting easier and more enjoyable, we encourage you to carefully read
all of the general instructions, study the color photographs, and familiarize
yourself with the individual project instructions before beginning a project.

QUILTING SUPPLIES

This list includes all the tools you need for basic quiltmaking, plus additional supplies used for special techniques. Unless otherwise specified, all items may be found in your favorite fabric store or quilt shop.

Batting — Batting is most commonly available in polyester, cotton, or a polyester/cotton blend (see **Choosing and Preparing the Batting**, page 108).

Cutting mat — A cutting mat is a special mat designed to be used with a rotary cutter. A mat that measures approximately 18" X 24" is a good size for most cutting.

Eraser — A soft white fabric eraser or white art eraser may be used to remove pencil marks from fabric. Do not use a colored eraser, as the dye may discolor fabric.

Freezer paper — This heavy, white paper with a wax coating on one side will adhere temporarily to fabric when pressed on with a dry iron.

Iron — An iron with both steam and dry settings and a smooth, clean soleplate is necessary for proper pressing.

Marking tools — There are many different marking tools available (see **Marking Quilting Lines**, page 107). A silver quilter's pencil is a good marker for both light and dark fabrics.

Masking tape — Two widths of masking tape, 1"w and 1/4"w, are helpful when quilting. The 1"w tape is used to secure the backing fabric to a flat surface when layering the quilt. The 1/4"w tape may be used as a guide when outline quilting.

Needles — Two types of needles are used for hand sewing: Betweens, used for quilting, are short and strong for stitching through layered fabric and batting. Sharps are longer, thinner needles used for basting and other hand sewing. For sewing machine needles, we recommend size 10 to 14 or 70 to 90 universal (sharp-pointed) needles.

Permanent fine-point pen — A permanent pen is used to mark templates and stencils and to sign and date quilts. Test pen on fabric to make sure it will not bleed or wash out.

Pins — Straight pins made especially for quilting are extra long with large round heads. Glass head pins will stand up to occasional contact with a hot iron. Some quilters prefer extra-fine dressmaker's silk pins. If you are machine quilting, you will need a large supply of 1" long (size 01) rustproof safety pins for pin-basting.

Quilting hoop or frame — Quilting hoops and frames are designed to hold the 3 layers of a quilt together securely while you quilt. Many different types and sizes are available, including round and oval wooden hoops, frames made of rigid plastic pipe, and large floor frames made of either material. A 14" or 16" hoop allows you to quilt in your lap and makes your quilting portable.

Rotary cutter — The rotary cutter is the essential tool for quick-method quilting techniques. The cutter consists of a round, sharp blade mounted on a handle with a retractable blade guard for safety. It should be used only with a cutting mat and rotary cutting ruler. We recommend the 45 mm size for most projects.

Rotary cutting ruler — A rotary cutting ruler is a thick, clear acrylic ruler made specifically for use with a rotary cutter. It should have accurate 1/8" crosswise and lengthwise markings and markings for 45° and 60° angles. A 6" X 24" ruler is a good size for most cutting. An additional 6" X 12" ruler or 12 1/2" square ruler is helpful when cutting wider pieces. Many specialty rulers are available that make specific cutting tasks faster and easier.

Scissors — Although most fabric cutting will be done with a rotary cutter, sharp, high-quality scissors are still needed for some cutting. A separate pair of scissors for cutting paper and plastic is recommended. Smaller scissors are handy for clipping threads.

Seam ripper — A good seam ripper with a fine point is useful for removing stitching.

Sewing machine — A sewing machine that produces a good, even straight stitch is all that is necessary for most quilting. Clean and oil your machine often and keep the tension set properly.

Tape measure — A flexible 120" long tape measure is helpful for measuring a quilt top before adding borders.

Template material — Sheets of translucent plastic, often pre-marked with a grid, are made especially for making quilting stencils.

Thimble — A thimble is necessary when hand quilting. Thimbles are available in metal, plastic, or leather and in many sizes and styles. Choose a thimble that fits well and is comfortable.

Thread — Several types of thread are used for quiltmaking: General-purpose sewing thread is used for basting and piecing. Choose high-quality cotton or cotton-covered polyester thread in light and dark neutrals, such as ecru and grey, for your basic supplies. Quilting thread is stronger than general-purpose sewing thread, and some brands have a coating to make them slide more easily through the quilt layers.

Triangle — A large plastic right-angle triangle (available in art and office supply stores) is useful in rotary cutting for making first cuts to "square up" raw edges of fabric and for checking to see that cuts remain at right angles to the fold.

Walking foot — A walking foot, or even-feed foot, is needed for straight-line machine quilting. This special foot will help all 3 layers move at the same rate over the feed dogs to provide a smoother quilted project.

FABRICS

Selecting Fabrics

Choose high-quality, medium-weight 100% cotton fabrics such as broadcloth or calico. All-cotton fabrics hold a crease better, fray less, and are easier to quilt than cotton/polyester blends. All the fabrics for a quilt should be of comparable weight and weave. Check the end of the fabric bolt for fiber content and width.

The yardage requirements listed for each project are based on 45" wide fabric with a "usable" width of 42" after shrinkage and trimming selvages. Your actual usable width will probably vary slightly from fabric to fabric. Though most fabrics will yield 42" or more, if you find a fabric that you suspect will yield a narrower usable width, you will need to purchase additional yardage to compensate. Our recommended yardage lengths should be adequate for occasional resquaring of fabric when many cuts are required, but it never hurts to buy a little more fabric for insurance against a narrower usable width, the occasional cutting error, or to have on hand for making coordinating projects.

Preparing Fabrics

All fabrics should be washed, dried, and pressed before cutting.

1. To check colorfastness before washing, cut a small piece of the fabric and place in a glass of hot water with a little detergent. Leave fabric in the water for a few minutes. Remove fabric from water and blot with white paper towels. If any color bleeds onto the towels, wash the fabric separately with warm water and detergent, then rinse until the water runs clear. If fabric continues to bleed, choose another fabric.

2. Unfold yardage and separate fabrics by color. To help reduce raveling, use scissors to snip a small triangle from each corner of your fabric pieces. Machine wash fabrics in warm water with a small amount of mild laundry detergent. Do not use fabric softener. Rinse well and then dry fabrics in the dryer, checking long fabric lengths occasionally to make sure they are not tangling.

3. To make ironing easier, remove fabrics from dryer while they are slightly damp. Refold each fabric lengthwise (as it was on the bolt) with wrong sides together and matching selvages. If necessary, adjust slightly at selvages so that fold lays flat. Press each fabric using a steam iron set on "Cotton."

ROTARY CUTTING

Based on the idea that you can easily cut strips of fabric and then cut those strips into smaller pieces, rotary cutting has brought speed and accuracy to quiltmaking. Observe safety precautions when using the rotary cutter, since it is extremely sharp. Develop a habit of retracting the blade guard just before making a cut and closing it immediately afterward, before laying down the cutter.

1. Follow **Preparing Fabrics**, page 101, to wash, dry, and press fabrics.

2. Cut all strips from the selvage-to-selvage width of the fabric unless otherwise indicated in project instructions. Place fabric on the cutting mat, as shown in **Fig. 1**, with the fold of the fabric toward you. To straighten the uneven fabric edge, make the first "squaring up" cut by placing the right edge of the rotary cutting ruler over the left raw edge of the fabric. Place right-angle triangle (or another rotary cutting ruler) with the lower edge carefully aligned with the fold and the left edge against the ruler (**Fig. 1**). Hold the ruler firmly with your left hand, placing your little finger off the left edge to anchor the ruler. Remove the triangle, pick up the rotary cutter, and retract the blade guard. Using a smooth downward motion, make the cut by running the blade of the rotary cutter firmly along the right edge of the ruler (**Fig. 2**). Always cut in a direction away from your body and immediately close the blade guard after each cut.

Fig. 1

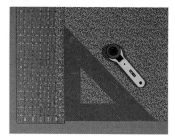

Fig. 2

3. To cut each of the strips required for a project, place the ruler over the cut edge of the fabric, aligning desired marking on the ruler with the cut edge (**Fig. 3**); make the cut. When cutting several strips from a single piece of fabric, it is important to occasionally use the ruler and triangle to ensure that cuts are still at a perfect right angle to the fold. If not, repeat Step 2 to straighten.

Fig. 3

4. To square up selvage ends of a strip before cutting pieces, refer to **Fig. 4** and place folded strip on mat with selvage ends to your right. Aligning a horizontal marking on ruler with 1 long edge of strip, use rotary cutter to trim selvage to make end of strip square and even (**Fig. 4**). Turn strip (or entire mat) so that cut end is to your left before making subsequent cuts.

Fig. 4

5. Pieces such as rectangles and squares can now be cut from strips. Usually strips remain folded, and pieces are cut in pairs after ends of strips are squared up. To cut squares or rectangles from a strip, place ruler over left end of strip, aligning desired marking on ruler with cut end of strip. To ensure perfectly square cuts, align a horizontal marking on ruler with 1 long edge of strip (**Fig. 5**) before making the cut.

Fig. 5

6. To cut 2 triangles from a square, cut square the size indicated in the project instructions. Cut square once diagonally to make 2 triangles (**Fig. 6**).

Fig. 6

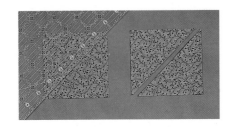

7. To cut 4 triangles from a square, cut square the size indicated in the project instructions. Cut square twice diagonally to make 4 triangles (**Fig. 7**). You may find it helpful to use a small rotary cutting mat so that the mat can be turned to make second cut without disturbing fabric pieces.

Fig. 7

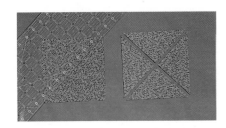

8. After some practice, you may want to try stacking up to 6 fabric layers when making cuts. When stacking strips, match long cut edges and follow Step 4 to square up ends of strip stack. Carefully turn stack (or entire mat) so that squared-up ends are to your left before making subsequent cuts. After cutting, check accuracy of pieces. Some shapes, such as diamonds, are more difficult to cut accurately in stacks.

9. In some cases, strips will be sewn together into strip sets before being cut into smaller units. When cutting a strip set, align a seam in strip set with a horizontal marking on the ruler to maintain square cuts (**Fig. 8**). We do not recommend stacking strip sets for rotary cutting.

Fig. 8

10. Most borders for quilts in this book are cut along the more stable lengthwise grain to minimize wavy edges caused by stretching. To remove selvages before cutting lengthwise strips, place fabric on mat with selvages to your left and squared-up end at bottom of mat. Placing ruler over selvage and using squared-up edge instead of fold, follow Step 2 to cut away selvages as you did raw edges (**Fig. 9**). After making a cut the length of the mat, move the next section of fabric to be cut onto the mat. Repeat until you have removed selvages from required length of fabric.

Fig. 9

11. After removing selvages, place ruler over left edge of fabric, aligning desired marking on ruler with cut edge of fabric. Make cuts as in Step 3. After each cut, move next section of fabric onto mat as in Step 10.

PIECING AND PRESSING
Precise cutting, followed by accurate piecing and careful pressing, will ensure that all the pieces of your quilt top fit together well.

Piecing
Set sewing machine stitch length for approximately 11 stitches per inch. Use a new, sharp needle suited for medium-weight woven fabric.

Use a neutral-colored general-purpose sewing thread (not quilting thread) in the needle and in the bobbin. Stitch first on a scrap of fabric to check upper and bobbin thread tension; make any adjustments necessary.

For good results, it is **essential** that you stitch with an **accurate** 1/4" **seam allowance**. On many sewing machines, the measurement from the needle to the outer edge of the presser foot is 1/4". If this is the case with your machine, the presser foot is your best guide. If not, measure 1/4" from the needle and mark throat plate with a piece of masking tape. Special presser feet that are exactly 1/4" wide are also available for most sewing machines.

When piecing, **always** place pieces **right sides together** and **match raw edges**; pin if necessary. (If using straight pins, remove the pins just before they reach the sewing machine needle.)

Chain Piecing

Chain piecing whenever possible will make your work go faster and will usually result in more accurate piecing. Stack the pieces you will be sewing beside your machine in the order you will need them and in a position that will allow you to easily pick them up. Pick up each pair of pieces, carefully place them together as they will be sewn, and feed them into the machine one after the other. Stop between each pair only long enough to pick up the next and don't cut thread between pairs (**Fig. 10**). After all pieces are sewn, cut threads, press, and go on to the next step, again chain piecing when possible.

Fig. 10

Sewing Across Seam Intersections

When sewing across the intersection of 2 seams, place pieces right sides together and match seams exactly, making sure seam allowances are pressed in opposite directions (**Fig. 11**). To prevent fabric from shifting, you may wish to pin in place.

Fig. 11

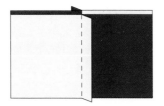

Sewing Bias Seams

Care should be used in handling and stitching bias edges since they stretch easily. After sewing the seam, carefully press seam allowance to 1 side, making sure not to stretch fabric.

Sewing Sharp Points

To ensure sharp points when joining triangular or diagonal pieces, stitch across the center of the "X" (shown in pink) formed on the wrong side by previous seams (**Fig. 12**).

Fig. 12

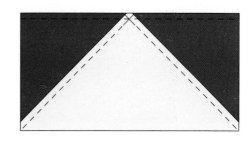

Trimming Seam Allowances

When sewing with triangle pieces, some seam allowances may extend beyond the edges of the sewn pieces. Trim away "dog ears" that extend beyond the edges of the sewn pieces (**Fig. 13**).

Fig. 13

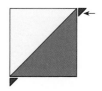

Pressing

Use a steam iron set on "Cotton" for all pressing. Press as you sew, taking care to prevent small folds along seamlines. Seam allowances are almost always pressed to one side, usually toward the darker fabric. However, to reduce bulk it may occasionally be necessary to press seam allowances toward the lighter fabric or even to press them open. In order to prevent a dark fabric seam allowance from showing through a light fabric, trim the darker seam allowance slightly narrower than the lighter seam allowance. To press long seams, such as those in long strip sets, without curving or other distortion, lay strips across the width of the ironing board.

MAKING TEMPLATES

Patterns for piecing templates include seam allowances; those for appliqué do not. To make a template from a pattern, use a permanent fine-point marker or pen to carefully trace the pattern onto template plastic, making sure to label the template and to transfer any alignment or grain line markings. Some patterns have multiple pieces (e.g., pattern pieces labeled A1 and A2). Match dashed lines and arrows to trace a complete pattern. Cut out template along drawn line. Check your template against the original pattern for accuracy.

APPLIQUÉ
Needle-Turn Appliqué

In this traditional hand appliqué method, the needle is used to turn the seam allowance under as you sew the appliqué to the background fabric using a Blind Stitch. When stitching, match the color of thread to the color of appliqué to disguise your stitches. Appliqué each piece starting with the ones directly on the background fabric. It is not necessary to appliqué areas that will be covered by another appliqué. Stitches on the right side of fabric should not show. Stitches on the edge of an appliqué and on background fabric should be equal in length. Clipped areas should be secured with a few extra stitches to prevent fraying.

1. Place template on right side of appliqué fabric. Use a pencil to lightly draw around template, leaving at least ¹/₂" between shapes; repeat for number of shapes specified in project instructions.

2. Cut out shapes approximately ³/₁₆" outside drawn line. Clip inside curves and points up to, but not through, drawn line. Arrange shapes on background fabric and pin or baste in place.

3. Thread a sharps needle with a single strand of general-purpose sewing thread; knot one end.

4. Pin center of appliqué to right side of background fabric. Begin on as straight an edge as possible and use point of needle to turn under a small amount of seam allowance, concealing drawn line on appliqué. Hold seam allowance in place with thumb of your non-sewing hand (**Fig. 14**).

Fig. 14

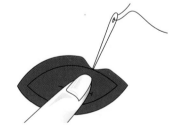

5. To stitch, bring needle up through background fabric at 1, even with turned edge of appliqué (**Fig. 15**).

Fig. 15

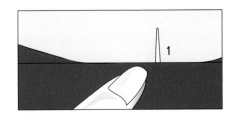

6. Insert needle into turned edge at 2, directly across from 1. Bring needle out of folded edge at 3 (**Fig. 16**). Insert needle into background fabric at 4, even with edge of appliqué and directly across from 3. Bring needle up through background fabric at 5, forming a small stitch on wrong side of fabric (**Fig. 17**).

Fig. 16

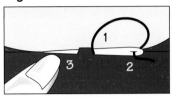

Fig. 17

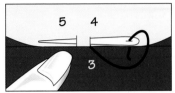

7. Continue needle-turning method to completely secure appliqué, referring to information below about stitching outward points and bias strips.

Stitching Outward Points: Appliqué long edge of shape until you are about ¹/₂" from the point (**Fig. 18**). Turn seam allowance under at point (**Fig. 19**). Turn remainder of seam allowance between stitching and point, using non-stitching thumb to hold allowance in place. Stitch to point, taking 2 or 3 stitches at top of point to secure. Turn under small amount of seam allowance past point and resume stitching.

Fig. 18

Fig. 19

Stitching Pressed Bias Strips: Since seam allowances have already been stitched or pressed under during preparation of bias strips used as appliqués, simply baste bias strip to background fabric, then stitch in place along edges using the same blindstitch used in needle-turning.

Fusible Appliqué

Patterns in this book are not printed in reverse. To use our speedy method of preparing appliqués, patterns must be reversed. White or light-colored fabrics may need to be lined with fusible interfacing before applying fusible web to prevent darker fabrics from showing through.

1. Place paper-backed fusible web, web side down, over appliqué pattern. Use a pencil to trace pattern onto paper side of web as many times as indicated in project instructions for a single fabric. Repeat for additional patterns and fabrics.

2. Follow manufacturer's instructions to fuse traced patterns to wrong side of fabrics. Do not remove paper backing. (Note: Some pieces may be given as measurements, such as a 2" x 4" rectangle, instead of drawn patterns. Fuse web to wrong side of the fabrics indicated for these pieces.)

3. Use scissors to cut out appliqué pieces along traced lines; use rotary cutting equipment to cut out appliqué pieces given as measurements. Remove paper backing from all pieces.

Satin Stitch Appliqué

A good satin stitch is a thick, smooth, almost solid line of zigzag stitching that covers the exposed raw edges of appliqué pieces.

1. Place a stabilizer, such as paper or any of the commercially available products, on wrong side of background fabric before stitching appliqués in place.

2. Thread needle of sewing machine with general-purpose thread. Use thread that matches the background fabric in the bobbin for all stitching. Set sewing machine for a medium width zigzag stitch (approximately $1/8$") and a very short stitch length. Set upper tension slightly looser than for regular stitching.

3. Beginning on as straight an edge as possible, position fabric so that most of the satin stitch will be on the appliqué piece. Do not backstitch; hold upper thread toward you and sew over it two or three stitches to anchor thread. Following Steps 4–7 for stitching corners and curves, stitch over exposed raw edges of appliqué pieces, changing thread color as necessary.

4. (*Note: Dots on **Figs. 20 - 25** indicate where to leave needle in fabric when pivoting.*) For **outside corners**, stitch just past the corner, stopping with the needle in **background** fabric (**Fig. 20**). Raise presser foot. Pivot project, lower presser foot, and stitch adjacent side (**Fig. 21**).

Fig. 20   Fig. 21

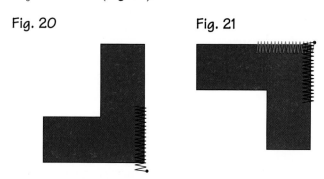

5. For **inside** corners, stitch just past the corner, stopping with the needle in **appliqué** fabric (**Fig. 22**). Raise presser foot. Pivot project, lower presser foot, and stitch adjacent side (**Fig. 23**).

Fig. 22   Fig. 23

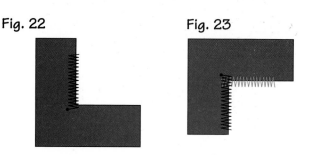

6. When stitching **outside** curves, stop with needle in **background** fabric. Raise presser foot and pivot project as needed. Lower presser foot and continue stitching, pivoting as often as necessary to follow curve (**Fig. 24**).

Fig. 24

7. When stitching **inside** curves, stop with needle in **appliqué** fabric. Raise presser foot and pivot project as needed. Lower presser foot and continue stitching, pivoting as often as necessary to follow curve (**Fig. 25**).

Fig. 25

8. Do not backstitch at end of stitching. Pull threads to wrong side of background fabric; knot thread and trim ends. Remove paper and stabilizer.

Cutting Away Fabric From Behind Appliqués

Hand quilting an appliquéd block will be easier if you are stitching through as few layers as possible. For this reason, or just to reduce bulk in your quilt, you may wish to cut away the background fabric behind appliqués. After stitching appliqués in place, turn block over and use sharp scissors or specially-designed appliqué scissors to trim away background fabric approximately $3/16$" from stitching line. Take care not to cut appliqué fabric or stitches.

BORDERS

Borders cut along the lengthwise grain will lie flatter than borders cut along the crosswise grain. Cutting lengths given for borders in this book are exact. You may wish to add an extra 2" of length at each end for "insurance"; borders will be trimmed after measuring completed center section of quilt top.

Adding Squared Borders

1. Mark the center of each edge of quilt top.
2. Most of the borders in this book have the side borders added first. To add side borders, measure across center of quilt top to determine length of borders (**Fig. 26**). Trim side borders to the determined length.

Fig. 26

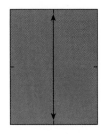

3. Mark center of 1 long edge of side border. Matching center marks and raw edges, pin border to quilt top, easing in any fullness; stitch. Repeat for other side border.
4. Measure center of quilt top, including attached borders, to determine length of top and bottom borders. Trim top and bottom borders to the determined length. Repeat Step 3 to add borders to quilt top (**Fig. 27**).

Fig. 27

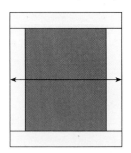

QUILTING

*Quilting holds the 3 layers (top, batting, and backing) of the quilt together and can be done by hand or machine. Our project instructions tell you which method is used on each project and show you quilting diagrams that can be used as suggestions for marking quilting designs. Because marking, layering, and quilting are interrelated and may be done in different orders depending on circumstances, please read the entire **Quilting** section, pages 107 - 110, before beginning the quilting process on your project.*

Types Of Quilting
In the Ditch

Quilting very close to a seamline or appliqué is called "in the ditch" quilting. This type of quilting does not need to be marked. When quilting in the ditch, quilt on the side **opposite** the seam allowance.

Outline Quilting

Quilting approximately 1/4" from a seam or appliqué is called "outline" quilting. Outline quilting may be marked, or you may place 1/4"w masking tape along seamlines and quilt along the opposite edge of the tape. (Do not leave tape on quilt longer than necessary, since it may leave an adhesive residue.)

Marking Quilting Lines

Fabric marking pencils, various types of chalk markers, and fabric marking pens with inks that disappear with exposure to air or water are readily available and work well for different applications. Lead pencils work well on light-color fabrics, but marks may be difficult to remove. White pencils work well on dark-color fabrics, and silver pencils show up well on many colors. Since chalk rubs off easily, it's a good choice if you are marking as you quilt. Fabric marking pens make more durable and visible markings, but the marks should be carefully removed according to manufacturer's instructions. Press down only as hard as necessary to make a visible line.

When you choose to mark your quilt, whether before or after the layers are basted together, is also a factor in deciding which marking tool to use. If you mark with chalk or a chalk pencil, handling the quilt during basting may rub off the markings. Intricate or ornamental designs may not be practical to mark as you quilt; mark these designs before basting using a more durable marker.

To choose marking tools, take all these factors into consideration and test different markers on scrap fabric until you find the one that gives the desired result.

Using Quilting Stencils

A wide variety of precut quilting stencils, as well as entire books of quilting patterns, are available. Using a stencil makes it easier to mark intricate or repetitive designs on your quilt top.

1. To make a stencil from a pattern, center template plastic over pattern and use a permanent marker to trace pattern onto plastic.
2. Use a craft knife with a single or double blade to cut narrow slits along traced lines (**Fig. 28**).

Fig. 28

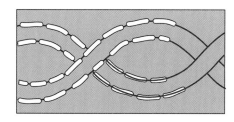

3. Use desired marking tool and stencil to mark quilting lines.

Choosing and Preparing the Backing

To allow for slight shifting of the quilt top during quilting, the backing should be approximately 4" larger on all sides for a bed-size quilt top or approximately 2" larger on all sides for a wall hanging. Yardage requirements listed for quilt backings are calculated for 45"w fabric. If you are making a bed-size quilt, using 90"w or 108"w fabric for the backing may eliminate piecing. To piece a backing using 45"w fabric, use the following instructions.

1. Measure length and width of quilt top; add 8" (4" for a wall hanging) to each measurement.
2. If quilt top is 76"w or less, cut backing fabric into 2 lengths slightly longer than the determined length measurement. Trim selvages. Place lengths with right sides facing and sew long edges together, forming a tube (**Fig. 29**). Match seams and press along 1 fold (**Fig. 30**). Cut along pressed fold to form a single piece (**Fig. 31**).

Fig. 29   **Fig. 30**   **Fig. 31**

 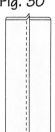 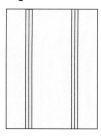

3. If quilt top is more than 76"w, cut backing fabric into 3 lengths slightly longer than the determined width measurement. Trim selvages. Sew long edges together to form a single piece.
4. Trim backing to correct size, if necessary, and press seam allowances open.

Choosing and Preparing the Batting

Choosing the right batting will make your quilting job easier. For fine hand quilting, choose a low-loft batting in any of the fiber types described here. Machine quilters will want to choose a low-loft batting that is all cotton or a cotton/polyester blend because the cotton helps "grip" the layers of the quilt. If the quilt is to be tied, a high-loft batting, sometimes called extra-loft or fat batting, is a good choice.

Batting is available in many different fibers. Bonded polyester batting is one of the most popular batting types. It is treated with a protective coating to stabilize the fibers and to reduce "bearding," a process in which batting fibers work their way out through the quilt fabrics. Other batting options include cotton/polyester batting, which combines the best of both polyester and cotton battings; all-cotton batting, which must be quilted more closely than polyester batting; and wool and silk battings, which are generally more expensive and usually only dry-cleanable.

Whichever batting you choose, read the manufacturer's instructions closely for any special notes on care or preparation. When you're ready to use your chosen batting in a project, cut batting the same size as the prepared backing.

Assembling the Quilt

1. Examine wrong side of quilt top closely; trim any seam allowances and clip any threads that may show through the front of the quilt. Press quilt top.
2. If quilt top is to be marked before layering, mark quilting lines (see **Marking Quilting Lines**, page 107).
3. Place backing **wrong** side up on a flat surface. Use masking tape to tape edges of backing to surface. Place batting on top of backing fabric. Smooth batting gently, being careful not to stretch or tear. Center quilt top right side up on batting.
4. If hand quilting, begin in the center and work toward the outer edges to hand baste all layers together. Use long stitches and place basting lines approximately 4" apart (**Fig. 32**). Smooth fullness or wrinkles toward outer edges.

Fig. 32

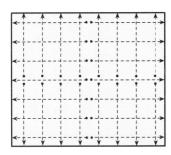

5. If machine quilting, use 1" rustproof safety pins to "pin-baste" all layers together, spacing pins approximately 4" apart. Begin at the center and work toward the outer edges to secure all layers. If possible, place pins away from areas that will be quilted, although pins may be removed as needed when quilting.

Hand Quilting

The quilting stitch is a basic running stitch that forms a broken line on the quilt top and backing. Stitches on the quilt top and backing should be straight and equal in length.

1. Secure center of quilt in hoop or frame. Check quilt top and backing to make sure they are smooth. To help prevent puckers, always begin quilting in the center of the quilt and work toward the outside edges.
2. Thread needle with an 18"-20" length of quilting thread; knot 1 end. Using a thimble, insert needle into quilt top and batting approximately 1/2" from where you wish to begin quilting. Bring needle up at the point where you wish to begin (**Fig. 33**); when knot catches on quilt top, give thread a quick, short pull to "pop" knot through fabric into batting (**Fig. 34**).

Fig. 33   Fig. 34

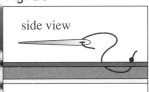   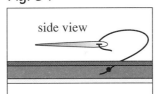

side view   side view

3. Holding the needle with your sewing hand and placing your other hand underneath the quilt, use thimble to push the tip of the needle down through all layers. As soon as needle touches your finger underneath, use that finger to push the tip of the needle only back up through the layers to top of quilt. (The amount of the needle showing above the fabric determines the length of the quilting stitch.) Referring to **Fig. 35**, rock the needle up and down, taking 3 - 6 stitches before bringing the needle and thread

completely through the layers. Check the back of the quilt to make sure stitches are going through all layers. When quilting through a seam allowance or quilting a curve or corner, you may need to make 1 stitch at a time.

Fig. 35

4. When you reach the end of your thread, knot thread close to the fabric and "pop" knot into batting; clip thread close to fabric.
5. Stop and move your hoop as often as necessary. You do not have to tie a knot every time you move your hoop; you may leave the thread dangling and pick it up again when you return to that part of the quilt.

Machine Quilting

The following instructions are for straight-line quilting, which requires a walking foot or even-feed foot. The term "straight-line" is somewhat deceptive, since curves (especially gentle ones) as well as straight lines can be stitched with this technique.

1. Wind your sewing machine bobbin with general-purpose thread that matches the quilt backing. Do not use quilting thread. Thread the needle of your machine with transparent monofilament thread if you want your quilting to blend with your quilt top fabrics. Use decorative thread, such as a metallic or contrasting-color general-purpose thread, when you want the quilting lines to stand out more. Set the stitch length for 6 - 10 stitches per inch and attach the walking foot to sewing machine.
2. After pin-basting, decide which section of the quilt will have the longest continuous quilting line, oftentimes the area from center top to center bottom. Leaving the area exposed where you will place your first line of quilting, roll up each edge of the quilt to help reduce the bulk, keeping fabrics smooth. Smaller projects may not need to be rolled.
3. Start stitching at beginning of longest quilting line, using very short stitches for the first 1/4" to "lock" beginning of quilting line. Stitch across project, using one hand on each side of the walking foot to slightly spread the fabric and to guide the fabric through the machine. Lock stitches at end of quilting line.

4. Continue machine quilting, stitching longer quilting lines first to stabilize the quilt before moving on to other areas.

Machine Stipple Quilting

The term, "stipple quilting," refers to dense quilting using a meandering line of machine stitching or closely spaced hand stitching.

1. Wind your sewing machine bobbin with general-purpose thread that matches the quilt backing. Do not use quilting thread. Thread the needle of your machine with transparent monofilament thread if you want your quilting to blend with your quilt top fabrics. Use decorative thread, such as a metallic or contrasting-colored general-purpose thread, when you want the quilting lines to stand out more.

2. For random stipple quilting, use a darning foot, drop or cover feed dogs, and set stitch length at zero. Pull up bobbin thread and hold both thread ends while you stitch 2 or 3 stitches in place to lock thread. Cut threads near quilt surface. Place hands lightly on quilt on either side of darning foot.

3. Begin stitching in a meandering pattern (**Fig. 36**), guiding the quilt with your hands. The object is to make stitches of similar length and to not sew over previous stitching lines. The movement of your hands is what determines the stitch length; it takes practice to coordinate your hand motions and the pressure you put on the foot pedal, so go slowly at first.

Fig. 36

4. Continue machine quilting, filling in one open area of the quilt before moving on to another area, locking thread again at end of each line of stitching by sewing 2 or 3 stitches in place and trimming thread ends.

BINDING

Binding encloses the raw edges of your quilt. Because of its stretchiness, bias binding works well for binding projects with curves or rounded corners and tends to lie smooth and flat in any given circumstance. It is also more durable than other types of binding.

Making Continuous Bias Strip Binding

Bias strips for binding can simply be cut and pieced to the desired length. However, when a long length of binding is needed, the "continuous" method is quick and accurate.

1. Cut a square from binding fabric the size indicated in the project instructions. Cut square in half diagonally to make 2 triangles.

2. With right sides together and using a 1/4" seam allowance, sew triangles together (**Fig. 37**); press seam allowance open.

Fig. 37

3. On wrong side of fabric, draw lines the width of the binding as specified in the project instructions, usually 2½" (**Fig. 38**). Cut off any remaining fabric less than this width.

Fig. 38

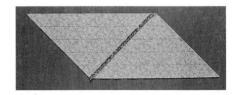

4. With right sides inside, bring short edges together to form a tube; match raw edges so that first drawn line of top section meets second drawn line of bottom section (**Fig. 39**).

Fig. 39

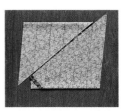

5. Carefully pin edges together by inserting pins through drawn lines at the point where drawn lines intersect, making sure the pins go through intersections on both sides. Using a 1/4" seam allowance, sew edges together. Press seam allowance open.

6. To cut continuous strip, begin cutting along first drawn line (**Fig. 40**). Continue cutting along drawn line around tube.

Trim ends of bias strip square.

Matching wrong sides and raw edges, press bias strip in half lengthwise to complete binding.

Attaching Binding With Mitered Corners

Press 1 end of binding diagonally (**Fig. 41**).

Fig. 41

Beginning with pressed end several inches from a corner, lay binding around quilt to make sure that seams in binding will not end up at a corner. Adjust placement if necessary. Matching raw edges of binding to raw edge of quilt top, pin binding to right side of quilt along 1 edge.

When you reach the first corner, mark ¹/₄" from corner of quilt top (**Fig. 42**).

Fig. 42

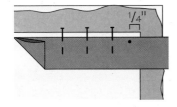

Using a ¹/₄" seam allowance, sew binding to quilt, backstitching at beginning of stitching and when you reach the mark (**Fig. 43**). Lift needle out of fabric and clip thread.

Fig. 43

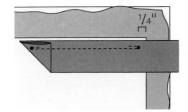

5. Fold binding as shown in **Figs. 44** and **45** and pin binding to adjacent side, matching raw edges. When you reach the next corner, mark ¹/₄" from edge of quilt top.

Fig. 44   **Fig. 45**

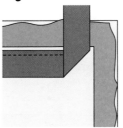   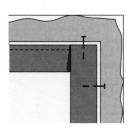

6. Backstitching at edge of quilt top, sew pinned binding to quilt (**Fig. 46**); backstitch when you reach the next mark. Lift needle out of fabric and clip thread.

Fig. 46

7. Repeat Steps 5 and 6 to continue sewing binding to quilt until binding overlaps beginning end by approximately 2". Trim excess binding.

8. If using 2¹/₂"w binding (finished size ¹/₂"), trim backing and batting a scant ¹/₄" larger than quilt top so that batting and backing will fill the binding when it is folded over to the quilt backing. If using narrower binding, trim backing and batting even with edges of quilt top.

9. On 1 edge of quilt, fold binding over to quilt backing and pin pressed edge in place, covering stitching line (**Fig. 47**). On adjacent side, fold binding over, forming a mitered corner (**Fig. 48**). Repeat to pin remainder of binding in place.

Fig. 47   **Fig. 48**

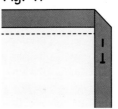   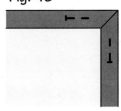

10. Blindstitch binding to backing, taking care not to stitch through to front of quilt.

Blindstitch

Come up at 1. Go down at 2 and come up at 3. Length of stitches may be varied as desired.

Fig. 49

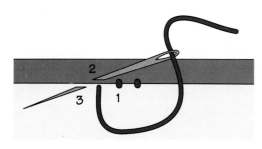

MAKING A HANGING SLEEVE

Attaching a hanging sleeve to the back of your wall hanging or quilt before the binding is added allows you to display your completed project on a wall.

1. Measure the width of the wall hanging top and subtract 1". Cut a piece of fabric 7"w by the determined measurement.

2. Press short edges of fabric piece ¼" to wrong side; press edges ¼" to wrong side again and machine stitch in place.

3. Matching wrong sides, fold piece in half lengthwise to form a tube.

4. Follow project instructions to sew binding to quilt top and to trim backing and batting. Before blindstitching binding to backing, match raw edges and stitch hanging sleeve to center top edge on back of wall hanging.

5. Finish binding wall hanging, treating the hanging sleeve as part of the backing.

6. Blindstitch bottom of hanging sleeve to backing, taking care not to stitch through to front of quilt.

7. Insert dowel or slat into hanging sleeve.

SIGNING AND DATING YOUR QUILT

Your completed quilt is a work of art and should be signed and dated. There are many different ways to do this, and you should pick a method that reflects the style of the quilt, the occasion for which it was made, and your own particular talents.

The following suggestions may give you an idea for recording the history of your quilt for future generations.

- Embroider your name, the date, and any additional information on the quilt top or backing. You may choose embroidery floss colors that closely match the fabric you are working on, such as white floss on a white border, or contrasting colors may be used.

- Make a label from muslin and use a permanent marker to write your information. Your label may be as plain or as fancy as you wish. Stitch the label to the back of the quilt.

- Chart a cross-stitch label design that includes the information you wish and stitch it in colors that complement the quilt. Stitch the finished label to the quilt backing.

METRIC CONVERSION CHART

Metric Conversion Chart

Inches x 2.54 = centimeters (cm)	Yards x .9144 = meters (m)
Inches x 25.4 = millimeters (mm)	Yards x 91.44 = centimeters (cm)
Inches x .0254 = meters (m)	Centimeters x .3937 = inches (")
	Meters x 1.0936 = yards (yd)

Standard Equivalents

⅛"	3.2 mm	0.32 cm	⅛ yard	11.43 cm	0.11 m
¼"	6.35 mm	0.635 cm	¼ yard	22.86 cm	0.23 m
⅜"	9.5 mm	0.95 cm	⅜ yard	34.29 cm	0.34 m
½"	12.7 mm	1.27 cm	½ yard	45.72 cm	0.46 m
⅝"	15.9 mm	1.59 cm	⅝ yard	57.15 cm	0.57 m
¾"	19.1 mm	1.91 cm	¾ yard	68.58 cm	0.69 m
⅞"	22.2 mm	2.22 cm	⅞ yard	80 cm	0.8 m
1"	25.4 mm	2.54 cm	1 yard	91.44 cm	0.91 m

We have made every effort to ensure that these instructions are accurate and complete. We cannot, however, be responsible for human error, typographical mistakes, or variations in individual work.

Softcover ISBN1-57486-327-4

Production Team: Technical Writers – Jean Lewis and Frances Huddleston; Editorial Writer – Kimberly L. Ross; Lead Graphic Artist – Dana Vaughn: Graphic Artists – Rebecca Hester and Dayle Cosh; Photographer – Andrew Uilkie; Photography Stylist – Cassie Newsome.